To [signature]

The Face Of Forgiveness

A Memoir

by

Rev. Dr. Johannes J. Christian

BRENTWOOD CHRISTIAN PRESS
Columbus, Georgia USA
2005

The Face Of Forgiveness: A Memoir

© 2005 Rev. Dr. Johannes J. Christian

ISBN 978-1477520871

No part of this publication may be reproduced in any material form (including photocopying or storing in any medium by electronic means and whether or not transiently or incidentally to some other use of this publication) without the written permission of the copyright holder, except in accordance with the provision of the Copyright, Designs and Patents Act 1988.

Additional copies of *The Face Of Forgiveness* may be ordered directly from:

Rev. Dr. Johannes J. Christian
POB 27463
Columbus OH 43227-3535 USA

Phone: +1-614-253-7385
www.DocChristian.com
www.FaceOfForgiveness.com

Jacket Design: 2005 by Earl Boxer Creations. Photo (c) 2005 by Chris Stewart/ *Dayton Daily News*. Any other usage requires written permission of photographer.
Other photos: Personal collection of Rev. Dr. Johannes J. Christian.
Proofreading, technical and spiritual support: Dondrea Rio Brown, Amanda Crosby and Shirley E. Butler

       Library of Congress Cataloging-in-Publication Data

Christian, Johannes J. 1950 –

       The Face Of Forgiveness / by Rev Dr Johannes J Christian with JC Phillips
       p.cm.
       ISBN **1-59581-210-5** (alk. paper)
I. Christian, Johannes J Christian, 1950 – 2. Pastors – US – Biography. I. Title: The Face Of Forgiveness. II. Jeffrey c. Phillips, 1962 – III. Title.

This book is dedicated to:

- ✟ My parents, George and Shirley Christian
- ✟ All of those people in various places who have fostered my healing process
- ✟ The membership of Adoration and Peace Baptist Church, Columbus OH
- ✟ Glenn and Patricia Phillips of New Middletown, Ohio, who are responsible for bringing Jeff into my life. He is my friend, my confidant, my wordsmith and my publicist, and...
- ✟ Sandra T. Kleckley, for her support, encouragement, and car given to me through this endeavor

REGIONAL HEADLINES
Byline: Compiled from Staff Reports
Date: September 15, 2001
Publication: *Dayton Daily News* (OH)
Edition: City
Section: Local
Page: 2B

Teen's case sent to adult court

SPRINGFIELD - A teen-age boy's fascination with death and his "callous disregard for others" was enough to send his case to adult court, a judge ruled Friday.

Jacob C. McNary, 15, ... is accused of dropping a rock off an Interstate 70 overpass Aug. 9 that smashed a car windshield and hit a 50year-old motorist in the face. Clark County Juvenile Court Judge Joseph Monnin agreed with prosecutors, who argued this month that McNary should be tried as an adult.

"He is cold and uncaring. He is without direction or drive," Monnin wrote in his decision. "He abuses drugs, is antisocial, lacks self-control and fails to empathize."

McNary still could mature and succeed in life, Monnin said, but now is angry, irresponsible and dangerous to others.

"The youth's distrust of authority, his fascination with death and his callous disregard for others make it unlikely that he can benefit from rehabilitative services anytime soon," Monnin said.

Two of McNary's cousins testified at a hearing this month that they warned McNary, after he threw the first rock onto the highway that night, that he could kill someone.

"That's the point," he told them.

The second rock struck **Rev. Johannes J. Christian** of Columbus across the face and blinded him, possibly for life.

###

REGIONAL HEADLINES

Byline: Compiled from Staff Reports
Date: January 15, 2002
Publication: *Dayton Daily News* (OH)
Edition: City
Section: Local
Page: 2B

Rock-toss suspect rejects plea deal

SPRINGFIELD - A Harmony Twp. teen-ager accused of blinding a driver when he threw a rock off an overpass rejected a plea offer Monday.

Jacob C. McNary, 16, faces two counts each of attempted murder and felonious assault and one count of vandalism. He remains in the county jail in lieu of a $25,000 bond and is to be tried as an adult Jan. 28. Clark County Prosecutor Stephen A. Schumaker offered an undisclosed plea agreement, but McNary's public defender, Noel Kaech, turned it down during a pre-trial hearing Monday in Common Pleas Court. Schumaker would only say that he did not offer to reduce charges.

McNary is accused of throwing two 5- and 7-pound rocks off a highway overpass in Harmony Twp. The second smashed the windshield of an eastbound car on Interstate 70 and seriously injured the Rev. Johannes J. Christian, 51, of Columbus.

After the hearing, Christian, using a cane and holding a trachea plug in his throat to speak, said McNary's family had expressed their deep-felt sorrows. He said he felt sorry for the family and that he can forgive. Christian said he is going "day by day" and continues to require reconstructive surgery.

###

Table of Contents

Forward xi

Prologue 1

Christian Is My Name 9

Spiritual Warfare 31

"Okay, God, Take Me." 47

Finding Forgiveness 59

"I Will Survive" 91

Ripples of Life 105

First Steps 133

Future Steps 165

Governor signs rock-toss legislation

Byline: Diane Richey, Columbus Bureau
Date: January 9, 2003
Publication: *Dayton Daily News* (OH)

COLUMBUS - Gov. Bob Taft on Wednesday signed a bill increasing penalties for those who throw bricks, rocks or other objects from Ohio's bridges and highway overpasses.

The bill, sponsored by state Sen. Steve Austria, R-Beavercreek, stiffens penalties even if no one is injured. The act was a misdemeanor. Now it ranges from a fourth-degree misdemeanor for vehicular vandalism to a second-degree felony, if someone is seriously injured. As a second-degree felony, it carries a fine of up to $15,000 and a maximum of eight years in prison for a first-time offender, or 18 years if the defendant is a repeat violent offender.

The bill also creates a task force that will consider creating a rock-throwing awareness program for schools, (Austria) said. The group may also start a centralized database to identify high-risk spots and areas that may need protective fences.

"It happens more often that we realize," he said.

Austria proposed the bill after the **Rev. Johannes J. Christian** of Columbus was hit in the face July 9, 2001, by a large rock dropped from an overpass on Interstate 70 in Clark County. Christian lost his sight in the incident and needed several reconstructive surgeries.

Jacob McNary, who was 15 at the time the rock was dropped, pleaded guilty in adult court to attempted murder and began serving a 12-year prison sentence in February.

Christian stood by Taft's side as the bill was signed. Christian said he hopes the bill will curtail others from throwing objects from bridges.

His injury was a "great price to have to pay to see this legislation passed, "Taft said.

###

> "I can do all things through Christ who strengthens me."
>
> - Philippians 4:13

Forward

I was victimized the night of July 9, 2001, when a troubled juvenile tossed a 7-pound rock over a highway overpass near Springfield, Ohio. That rock crashed through the windshield of my car, onto my face, forever changing my life. I was permanently blinded and every bone from the top of my forehead to beneath my chin was pulverized. I would require 30 plastic surgeries to create something from where nothing remained.

I could have died that night. Doctors say I should have died that night. Since then, there have been moments I wish I had died that night. Death seems so easy, so convenient compared with the pain and torment that awaited my recovery, which continues today almost four years after the accident.

But something happened that sparked my will and my desire to live. I decided to use this experience to proclaim that I am a victim no more, to shout that I refuse to go quietly into the darkness and desolation of self-loathing and pity. I will forgive the man - the child, rather - that committed this most heinous act against me. I will not permit the evil forces, which placed him on that bridge that night, to claim power over my life.

As I made that determination, I could feel the energy, the grace and the mercy of God and our Lord, Jesus Christ, take control of my mind, my body and my soul. I knew I was preparing for a righteous purpose, the depth and breadth of which I still do not fully comprehend but welcome with open arms.

I will not be a victim. I refuse to be a victim. I am a survivor in the presence of our Lord, who died on the cross so that I may live. The body of Jesus Christ was destroyed on the cross, but not his spirit. My face was destroyed by a rock, but it did not touch my soul. If I am truly created in God's image, then the image I project today is of God. I refuse to be victim. My survival fueled a mission to spread the word of God with everyone I meet and everywhere I go. God is lighting my path, and I am following it. I pray others will join me. – *JJC*

Law raises punishment for 'game'

Byline: Mary McCarty
Date: January 12, 2003
Publication: *Dayton Daily-, News* (OH)
Edition: City
Section: Local Page: BI
Column: Mary McCarty Colunm

It was an act that nearly cost the Rev. Johannes Christian his life.

It was an act that robbed him of his sight, of the joy of watching his grandchildren open their presents on Christmas morning. Until Wednesday, that same act was on the books in Ohio as a misdemeanor.

Christian stood by Gov. Bob Taft's side Wednesday when he signed a bill increasing penalties: for those who throw rocks, bricks and other objects from Ohio's bridges and overpasses.

It's a long-overdue measure Christian hopes will prevent future tragedies.

"A misdemeanor is something that doesn't impact somebody's life - a youngster steals a pack of gum, an insignificant, lifeless item," Christian said. "I have had 30 surgeries in the past year-and-a-half bone transplants, skin grafts, plastic surgery, a complete nose job. And I still have no eyes. I have two prosthetic eyes, but that's just for show."

That being said, Christian feels lucky to be alive. A Mohrsville, Pa., mother of three wasn't So fortunate.

On Jan. 3, Elaine Cowell was driving back from a ski trip with her husband and three children when, on a stretch of highway in Bethlehem, Pa., an 18-pound chunk of ice smashed through the windshield of their van. That basketball-sized projectile instantly killed Cowell.

Investigators distributed hundreds of fliers at local high schools. More than 30 students responded, leading to the arrest Wednesday of Dennis Gumbs, 15, of Allentown, Pa.

It wasn't until July 9, 2001 that the state of Ohio started to take a serious look at the problem. That's when 15-year-old Jacob McNary dropped a large rock from an overpass on Interstate 70 in Clark County, striking Christian's car.

(Continued on Next Page)
(Continued from Previous Page)

"His case was very influential," said state Sen. Steve Austria, R-Beavercreek, who sponsored the bill.

The new penalty structure stiffens punishment even if there are no injuries. Now rock-tossing ranges from a fourth-degree misdemeanor to a second-degree felony in the case of serious injuries.

Perhaps more important, the bill provides for a central database that will let local law enforcement officials, state highway patrols, county engineers and the Ohio Department of Transportation identify problem overpasses. "Up til now, there was no coordination between agencies," Austria said.

The victim's brother, Arthur Christian of Urbana, discovered that there had been numerous incidents at the same overpass. "To this day the bridge is still not covered," he said. "I said to myself, 'This is crazy; this is insane.'

So he lobbied hard for the bill. "After the rock hit my brother, I was devastated," he said. "I wanted to do something."

The brothers think the bill is a step in the right direction.

"We haven't helped this generation coming behind us to understand how valuable people are," the Rev. Christian said. "We have video games training people to be snipers, or training someone how to shoot somebody."

###

The Face Of Forgiveness

A Memoir

By Rev. Dr. Johannes J. Christian

> "Be it known unto you therefore, men and brethren, that through this man is preached unto you the forgiveness of sins."
>
> *- Acts 13:38*

Prologue

From one of the most horrific and devastating events of my life, I received a most powerful lesson as well as a blessing from God, although I did not know it at that moment.

It was July 9, 2001, and I was returning home from a family gathering in Peoria, Ill., where my daughter, Vanessa, and her family reside. I had been with Vanessa, her husband, John, and their three children, to celebrate the dedication of their youngest son, John II. It had been a glorious day as I remember it, a sunshiny day in July. We picnicked with friends and relatives in their backyard in warm celebration. I had spent time playing with my grandchildren and some of their friends. Making the trip with me was my foster son, Brian Rinear, 16, who had been living with me for just four months. We were having so much fun that I lost track of time. Suddenly, in the late afternoon, we realized we needed to get on the road for the six-hour trip home to Columbus, Ohio.

For Brian and me, the journey had been filled with many opportunities to get to know one another better. Brian, who was one of some 30 foster children I've care for since the mid-1980s – nagged me about wanting to take his turn behind the wheel, which is natural for most 16 year olds. He teased and taunted me: "You drive like an old man. If you would let me behind the wheel, we'd probably be in Indianapolis already. I don't know why you won't let me drive? You know you're getting tired."

No way weakened by his jibes, I replied, "We'll get there when we get there. I'm doing just fine. I feel good." One time, I did respond that "I'll be glad when you get your permit so that you can get behind the wheel." In hindsight, it is a blessing that I did not relinquish the wheel, as it very well could have been Brian who was injured in the accident. I know what you are thinking, that maybe had I let Brian drive it would have changed my fate as well? Maybe. But would you want to take a chance at such a thing to happen to a young life, a life that had yet to begin realizing its potential? Not me. I know God intended for me to be in that particular time and place. I didn't know it then and believe me, I spend months fighting that reality, but I know it now. I firmly believe the events of that weekend were pre-ordained by God, and I'll explain why later.

Back to the trip. Brian and I agreed to take turns tuning the radio for entertainment. This way we both could get to listen to the kind of music we wanted to hear. I prefer gospel stations, while Brian wanted to hear popular music. This means he put up with my gospel and I put up with his hip-hop music. Yes, hip-hop, the kind that bounces you out of the seat and vibrates the windows. I may not have enjoyed his musical tastes, but I intended to honor the deal I made with this young man; it was an hour of my music, and then an hour of his music as the miles passed under the wheels of my late-model Cadillac. The only time I even attempted to change the rules of the game was when he fell asleep, giving me an opening to keep my music playing. As fate would have it, every time my hour was scheduled to end, he would be wide awake and my head would be pounding to syncopated, driving hip-hop beats. In addition to music, we also engaged in conversation. Since I was still getting to know Brian, I wanted him to share his views about life, school, his particular foster-care experiences, and his plans for the future. We discussed our weekend together, and I explained the significance and meaning of the dedication service in the church, and why it was so important for me to attend. Brian told me how much he enjoyed being part of my family, and asked if I had really mean it when I said he could go back and visit the daughter's family on his own sometime. I told him that I meant it, and he seem to appreciate the faith and trust I had in him. The picnic, the time with my family, and this portion of our journey home are all I remember prior to the accident.

The hour was getting late and I remember voicing the fact that we were about "one hour from home." That was important because I needed to pick up my other foster son before midnight. The last thing I truly remember is checking my watch and noticing it was just after 11 p.m. It was at that moment that my life literally faded to black forever. From out of nowhere, I remember hearing a deafening, sickening crash. I remember nothing else. The rest of the information I have of that night comes from what I've been told by Brian, my family, doctors, law enforcement officials, attorneys, and from sworn testimony in a subsequent court case.

At that moment, on a dark, rural section of Interstate 70 in Clark County, Ohio, an 7-pound rock about the size of a melon crashed through the windshield of my car and landed directly on my face and pulverizing it. I wasn't really unconscious, but my brain shut down so that I didn't remember the experience. From what I'm told, Brian reacted quickly and performed a very heroic act. Despite the confusion and the fear that must have consumed him, Brian was able to disengage the cruise control (which was set at 69 mph) and steer the car from the left hand lane to the right lane and onto the shoulder of the road. Then, he brought the car under control and stopped; in a ironic sense, he finally go this chance to drive that day. But I jest. Next, he checked to make sure I was still breathing. Brian told me several months later that this took a couple tries as he couldn't believe his eyes. My blood and pieces of bone and muscle from my face was splattered everywhere. One of my eyes were gone, and the other was hanging from a large hole where my face once was. Blood covered the dashboard, my seat, and even my cell phone, which Brian couldn't bring himself to pick up. He remembered that he had turned on his cell phone several days before, and this thought heightened his anxiety as he did not know if it was really activated. Seeing that it still had power, he got out of the car and called 9-1-1.

Outside of the car, he frantically screamed to the emergency operator that there had been an accident and that they needed to send an ambulance. His voice was so strained the operator thought Brian was a woman, as she tried to help him explain what was happening. After correcting the dispatcher about his gender, Brian told her that we were traveling east on Interstate 70, and were somewhere near Springfield, Ohio, about 30 minutes west of Columbus. Brian was reluctant to return to the car because of my appearance frightened him; he also wanted to remain outside to flag down anyone that could help. Brian said many cars whizzed by, but no one stopped to help. It is no surprise that Brian quite was relieved when help finally arrived. Although he had some trouble finding our car, a trooper from the Ohio Highway Patrol arrived within five minutes of the 9-1-1 dispatch.. The state trooper called for an ambulance, and I was rushed to a hospital in Springfield. Brian thought I was dead.

Amazingly, and in an act that stands as a testament as to why I regard Brian as my guardian angel, he was able to get another call out to his parents in Kentucky, and he and the police reached members of my family. Not knowing what had happened, my sisters, Jean and Elaine, rushed to Springfield from Columbus, as did my sons, Tyrone and George. No one outside of Brian knew many details about the accident at that time, and my family did not know what to expect regarding my medical condition. At that time, no one knew that the rock had been deliberately thrown from an overpass; my family initially believed a piece of the bridge had broken away and crashed into the car. I can only imagine their horror when they first saw me in the intensive care unit and began to comprehend the full extent of my injuries.

It didn't take long for the doctors in Springfield to realize that I needed to be moved to a trauma center. My injuries were far greater than what that particular hospital was able to treat, so I was air-flighted from the Springfield Hospital to the Trauma Center at Miami Valley Hospital in Dayton, Ohio. I'm sure the doctors in Springfield believed that, while the attempt was admirable, I would be dead soon. Even though I was somewhere between life and death, and even though there was so much excitement going on around me, I remember nothing. My mind has not allowed me to recall events from the accident, emergency surgeries, and some portions of my recovery. What I know is what those around me have shared since that fateful day, from newspaper accounts of the story, and from court testimony.

No, my life did not end with the accident, but it did not begin with it, either. Yes, my life changed in a dramatic, almost incomprehensible manner. A new chapter of my life began the moment an 7-pound rock shattered my windshield and my face. Even so, I believe it is important for you to know who I was before the accident, and who God is driving me to be afterwards. There are no more dawns for me, nor are there sunsets, from a visual perspective. What remains and grows each day is a burning, intrinsic desire and a drive to share the Word, the power and glory of our Lord, Jesus Christ with whomever will listen and wherever it will take me. I was an instrument of God before the accident, but I am truly a vessel for Him now. One of my favorite Bible passages states: "I can do all things through Christ who strengthens me." This passage from Philippians had a special meaning for me with regard to my childhood and early adult life, but has even greater meaning for me today. ✝

> "But if ye do not forgive, neither will your Father which is in heaven forgive your trespasses."
>
> - Mark 11:26

Christian Is My Name

I am the sixth of seven children born to two hard-working African-American parents who moved from Long Island to Upstate New York in the early 1950s. As I recall, my life always seemed a bit different from the other children of my family.

I was a sickly, frail child, and throughout most of my life I have suffered with asthma and allergies. I also was an extremely emotional child, and carried my feelings on my shirtsleeve, so to speak. I was very easily offended and often felt like I was misunderstood in many ways. Whether it was because of these issues or divine providence, I remember that, even at an early age, faith and spirituality were very important to me. My family attended churches in the Saratoga Springs area of New York State, and it was something I always cherished. Whether it was the singing, the preaching or the music, attending church always seemed to be something that settled my turbulent, troubled spirit.

As I discuss my childhood, it is essential that we create a picture of our Christian household. I was born Dec. 6, 1950 in Port Jefferson, Long Island to George and Shirley Christian. George Christian was a proud man of West Indian heritage. He was the son of Elama and Johannes Christian, who came to New York City from St. Thomas, West Indies, Virgin Islands. My grandmother was actually born in Aruba and raised there and moved to a small Dutch island of Saba as a young woman, and later left Saba to move to St. Thomas, Virgin Islands. My grandfather, whose name I carry, Johannes Josephus Christian, was raised in St. Croix, West Indies, and was a merchant seaman early in life. I'm told that he was very well known for his swimming abilities and deep sea diving, and was responsible for laying the cables on the bottom of the ocean floor.

My grandparents married in St. Thomas, West Indies, and had five children. My father, George Christian, was the first of their children to be born in the United States. My father was raised in New York City in the Bronx and attended mostly public schools, as did his brothers and sisters, three of whom remained in the West Indies and came to the States over a three-year period to join my grandparents.

My mother's father was Jacob Ellis, and his family emigrated to the United States from Jamaica. He was actually born here in the States and lived in Virginia, near the town of Louisa, where he met and married Virginia Wade. Jacob Ellis and Virginia Wade were married in Charlotte, N.C., and made their way to Amsterdam, New York. I'm told that Jacob was quite an entrepreneur in the early part of his life. He owned and operated a broom factory and had a successful delivery business. He hauled rugs for several of the rug manufacturers in the are around the Albany area. He also ran cardboard salvage business, collecting cardboard boxes from many large department stores in the Albany, Schenectady and Amsterdam areas. These boxes were re-bundled and recycled, which was quite a profitable business. They were an African-American family, quite well off, and built a beautiful home on the top of a hill in the Amsterdam area. There were eight children that lived in that home, including my mother, Shirley Wade Ellis. She carried my grandmother's maiden name has her middle name and, like her, I carry her father's first name as my middle name, or Johannes Jacob Christian.

As I said, I was born in Port Jefferson, Long Island and was the sixth of seven children. Soon after I was born, our family left the Long Island/Middle Island area. (We actually lived out near Patchogue, Long Island, which is in the center of the island.) At that time Long Island was a sparsely inhabited area. Many immigrants had moved out of New York City in the early 1900s when there was a lot of inexpensive land, so my grandparents had bought a piece of land and, over time, built a five-bedroom house.

Our family lived in another smaller house that my mother's father had helped her build. We didn't live there long, however, as my family moved to Upstate New York, closer to the area my mother had been raised. My parents made the move for two reasons, one was to leave the humid, damp climate of Long Island and the second was to pursue better employment opportunities. My parents scoured the Amsterdam and Albany areas, looking for a house that would be suitable for our large family. Finding none, they pursued a lead passed to them by some friends, who said there was a piece of land located about eight miles north of Saratoga on U.S. Route 50, which at that time was a major thoroughfare between Albany and Montreal.

There they found a partially finished basement in the Gansevoort area that had been started by a married couple who were of Mohawk Indian descent. (The Mohawk Indians were indigenous to that area of New York State.) The couple had actually divorced and never finished the house. So, before my first birthday, my family moved from a home on Long Island and into a basement. We lived there from the fall until the spring, when we were forced to move out rather abruptly after torrential rains flooded our basement home. We moved back when the rains cleared, and with the help from other members of both my parent's families we built a first floor over our basement. While no one in our immediate family was experienced or equipped for carpentry, everyone was willing to help and brought with them hammers and saws. Much of the lumber used was used or scrap wood my grandfather found on his cardboard recycling route, making deals with merchants he had business dealings. Additional scrap lumber was picked up from sawmills in the Saratoga Springs area. As you may have already guessed, it was a crude house at best with it's mismatched boards and crude architecture. Nevertheless, we had a home for the nine of us, if you want to call it that. We had no indoor plumbing so, needless to say, we had an outhouse that was built out behind the basement, and hand pumps for water.

We did not have electricity in the basement, but I remember we had it shortly after a first floor was completed. Our house was heated by a coal-burning potbelly stove that sat in the middle of the basement floor. I remember my siblings and I were constantly warned by our mother not to stand too close to the fire for fear of being burned. It's interesting to point out that this form of heat production was indicative of what many people had during that era in that area.

The Saratoga area experienced brutal winters, meaning we literally got tons of snow each year and sub-zero temperatures were the norm. It was brutally cold in our house, which was poorly insulated. Later in life, I learned that there was no insulation in most of the walls and in some places it might have been wood and cardboard covered with sheetrock. Planks of knotty pine were used as a decorative cover in our living room, or "front room," as we called it.

For better or for worse, we made the transition from the big city to rural America. Our new community was predominantly white; we were the only African-American family as far as I can remember. Our immediate neighbors were of Native American descent. A gentleman I knew only as "Mr. Bryant" owned the 100 or more acres around our property. We were the only family in the area that were not related to him, making us even more peculiar. Most of the families—the Bryants, the Bisses, and the Beagles—were really one family though marriage. Despite our differences, I must point out that, even as children, we were well received by the people in the immediate area. As we grew, they grew to love and respect our family, and we all considered one another friends.

My parents took jobs in the Albany area. My mother and father both worked in the Veteran's Administrative Hospital in the early 1950, and drove 40 miles each way to work. My mother worked as a nurse's aide and my father worked in the lab. Dad retired from the Veteran's Hospital in the early 1980s after more than 30 years of employment. My mother worked for the hospital for a short time before moving to an office job in one of the government arsenals in the Albany area. Later, she took a job with the U.S. Postal Service, where she was able to continue her tenure with the United States government. She retired from the U.S. Postal Service.

There was one more Christian child born after me, my brother, Arthur, after we moved Upstate in 1952. I now do not remember much of my childhood, but I know we struggled financially. I'm sure that some people considered us to be poor. My parents learned how to farm to provide extra food for the family. We had an acre of land and were able to put in a garden and grew a lot of our own vegetables during the summer months. This alone was quite a different experience for my father, who grew up on the streets of New York City. He wasn't very apt as a farmer, and had difficulty producing enough food to feed six of seven children who still lived at home. (My sister, Martha, lived with my mother's parents in Amsterdam.) It doesn't surprise me that he sought assistance. I still remember Mr. Bryant—a tall, stern Indian– being quite instrumental in teaching my father to plant and farm. I even remember how, when we were trying to sink a well, Mr. Bryant came over with a divining rod made of a weeping willow branch.

He held the branch loosely in his hand, and as the point of the "y" moved towards the ground, he was able to tell my father where to sink a pipe for a well. As history has often proven, some of the ways of the Native Americans are very accurate. As they sunk the pipe, sure enough, there was water where Mr. Bryant predicted, and a hand pump was installed. I attended kindergarten at what was then a centrally located school. While most of my brothers and sisters were going to a one-room school, I went by school bus, in 1955, to Schuylerville to start kindergarten. I spent just that first year in a central school, which I really don't remember very much of at all, except for the fact that it was a very long bus ride back and forth to the Schuylerville.

I do, however, remember my first grade experience, because it was during in the first grade where I began attending a one-room schoolhouse located about one mile from our house. I had an opportunity then to walk back and forth from school with my siblings and the other children in our community. In fact we kind of formed our own train. As we went down the road in the mornings, each house had three to four children, and we'd all run out and walk to school together.

The pupils of the one-room schoolhouse were children from most of the families in our area. I remember it looking like the school building on the popular 1970s television show, "The Walton's," with its clapboard siding, large front double doors, and long, narrow windows on either side. It was nestled in a cleared area near the woods. The school was heated by coal, and it had a coal bin in the basement. It did not have partitions, meaning students in first through sixth grade sat in one, open room.

All of the students had traditional desks that had a flap in the front and little openings underneath your chair to place your books. As the teacher taught particular grade levels, other students were asked to work independently, or were given recess and were able to play outside. As you can imagine, the building was quite chaotic at times. Older siblings had to baby-sit younger brother and sisters. Because there were seven of us, most of us were in school together until the sixth grade. After the sixth grade, we moved to a centrally located school in Schuylerville, about 16 miles east from our house. At that time, Schuylerville is a small, factory and milling community that thrived off of Hudson River commerce. Most of the people in the Schuylerville area were quite different from those of us that lived in the Gansevoort/North Umberland area. As I said, Schuylerville was a mill town with plenty of well-paying jobs, so the homes were much better that ours, so it was a little bit more industrial. It seemed like the people of Schuylerville were more metropolitan, compared with those of us from rural parts. These socio-economic difference made things difficult at times.

As a child I had much difficulty learning, even in the first and second grades. Schoolwork did not come easy to me. I had an awful lot of problems just reading and trying to comprehend. My mother was called to the school a number of times to meet with the teacher and principal to determine whether or not there was a need to put me in special education classes. It's quite ironic that as children there were four boys in my family and all four of us had to repeat at least one or two grades. I cannot speak for my brothers, but my academic challenges were due to the fact that I was dyslexic. While I was able to determine and point out to people that I mixed up letters, such as Vs and Ds, and Ps and Qs, and I wrote some of my numbers backwards, I had a very good command of the verbal language. I was able to articulate and speak, and even though I spoke with a little squeaky voice, I was able to speak quite clearly and could recall things in great detail. So as the teachers and principals would point out to my parents that I had some learning disabilities, and they felt they needed to put me in special education, my mother would counter with the fact that I seemed to be quite adept at remembering things. So it was through her insistence that I was maintained in mainstream classes and not reassigned to special education.

    This, however, meant that even as a child I not only would do work at school, but my mother would do home schooling as well early in the morning and late at night. She would wake me up and I would have to sit and write spelling words 100 times apiece before I left for school; we even did this in the summer. To her great dismay, she couldn't believe that I could be so difficult and continue to write a word backwards, or letters backward, and spell words wrong over and over again. I remember my fingers hurting from having to write and rewrite words that I would continue to misspell. It was quite the same with my numbers. I wrote numbers backwards. I always knew there was something wrong with me, but we did not understand what it was. Remember, this was the late 1950s and early 1960s, and there was still so much that educators and scientists had to learn about dyslexia, and there were no treatments available like today. Nevertheless, my mother was very consistent, very persistent, and extremely patient considering how frustrating it must have been for her. I remember that some of my "home work" was done by light of a kerosene lamp and sometimes it was done in a very cold room. At that time the house was heated either by coal or, later in my childhood, we had an oil furnace, which we used as long as there was money to have oil. When there wasn't enough money for the oil, then we would burn wood. Either way the lessons continued because education was very, very important for my mother. She knew that if her children got a solid education, that they could improve their standing in life and in the community.

Of course I didn't understand why education was so important to her at that time. My mother was an extremely intelligent, hard-working woman; she was also very opinionated as well as articulate, which is probably where I obtained the verbal skills that help me as a preacher. In fact, a lot of people referred to her as "Miss Boston" because she spoke so well. I believe some of her speaking skills and work ethic was due to the fact that she was not able to complete her education. She graduated from high school in Amsterdam and left to go to Gordon College in Boston, where it appeared that she had to drop out of college due to an unplanned pregnancy form her first marriage. So for her children, it was vitally important that all of us would succeed in graduating from high school. She did all that was in her power to bring that about. Sometimes, I feel guilty that I couldn't meet the exacting academic expectations during my childhood and was forced to repeat the third, fourth and fifth grades. In hindsight, these early struggles are probably what motivated me to pursue academic excellence as an adult and push me to earn my doctoral degree. Despite my scholastic struggles, I was always proud that I never missed a day of school as a child. Part of this was because my mother would send us to school even when we were sick. I always had perfect attendance, even though I didn't always have perfect grades. By the time I got to third grade, the one-room schoolhouse was closed and we were sent by bus to Schuylerville Central School System.

It was in Schuylerville where I recall being made aware of the fact that we were the only African-American family in the immediate area, and that the color of our skin was darker than that of the other children in our class. It is here where we also encountered the stain of prejudice for the first time. At that time, we weren't referred to as African-Americans; we were called "Negroes." Some people, however, preferred to use the derogatory word, "nigger," which shook me to my core the first time I heard it. Since most of the people of Schuylerville worked in the mills. The homes and the community were quite different from where we lived. We were not accustomed to having indoor water and central heating electric lights. I remember it being quite delightful to be able to be warm and be inside of a centrally lighted building when we were moved over to school in Schuylerville.

As I said, learning was very difficult for me. I vividly remember teachers being quite frustrated trying to work with me. I remember one teacher calling me "dumb" and "stupid," which really hurt my feelings at that time. I know that today, it would unheard if for a teacher to make those kinds of remarks to students. One day, my mother stepped in and had a meeting with my teacher to plead my case and ask for patience, insisting that I was not "dumb" or "stupid." The next day, while the teacher took more time with me, it was very evident that the meeting did not change her attitude toward me. As she helped me with a math problem, I still remember her saying, "Well, your mother says that you're not dumb or stupid, so you're going to sit here and learn this." Another memory I have is of our principal, Mr. Barrett, who never could seem to grasp the pronunciation of my first name. Instead of calling me Johannes, he called me "Jonus," and refused to say it correctly no matter how many times I corrected him and plead for him to get it right. Whether this error was related to some innate stubbornness or pure prejudice, I'll never know. I always suspected that, because of the difficulties my brothers and I had in school, that Mr. Barrett really believed African-American males were incapable of learning. My sisters, on the other hand, all graduated high school without having to repeat a grade, a fact I find quite curious. I don't know what that says about the society in which we live, but in my mind it has left an indelible mark. While it would not have been spoken out loud, I do believe my struggles and the struggles of my brothers only bolstered an overriding sentiment that African-American males could not learn as well as their Caucasian contemporaries.

But let's hasten on. While my memories of school are difficult, I do fondly remember a class field trip where we got to ride the train to Albany from Schuylerville. It's etched in my brain because I do not remember ever riding the train before or after that excursion. Mostly, the memories of my elementary school years are filled with trauma due to challenges in the classroom.

I did not enjoy going to school, and I really did not want to go to school. Compounding my scholastic issues was the fact that I was often sick. I suffered from asthma and allergies, so every time the weather changed I became very ill. I wheezed, coughed, sneezed, and constantly had runny noses. Compounding my medical issues was the fact that I was a very high-strung child, which caused me to be picked on by almost everyone, including my siblings. I was nicknamed "JJC News Reporter" by my brothers and sisters because I would inevitably have a story to tell to my parents about whoever did whatever was not in line with their wishes and directives before they went to work. So everybody in the house knew that, if they didn't follow the house rules, I would run to mom and dad and tell them everything. This caused me to be constantly harassed by my brothers and sisters when mom and dad weren't around. Now, I do not want to leave you with the impression that I was not loved, because I was loved and felt love. It's just that my siblings and I had a real love-hate relationship.

I do not remember having a lot of friends, which was probably due to my sometimes-irrational temperament and my challenges in school. This was especially true when we went to school in Schuylerville. Home was better, as I did make friends with a couple of the kids in our own neighborhood. One was Minard Morehouse, who lived on the other side of the swamp from our house, and Eric Biss, who's family lived in the hills. The Bisses seemed to be very different from our family, and I'm not talking about race. You see, Mr. Biss worked for General Foods, and his immediate family owned a trucking company, meaning they were quite affluent. I remember Eric and Minard coming over to my house and the three of us would go play outside. I was permitted to go to their houses, but we were never permitted to play inside for reasons I never considered. There was Jesse and Jimmy Freeper, who also lived down the street from us. In the evenings, you'd find a dozen or so young people in the field behind our house playing baseball. Now, we had one softball and only a handful of bats between our families, but that didn't seem to matter. Since I did not own a glove, I remember being afraid to catch the ball because it stung my hands. I usually let the ball fall to the ground and pick it up before making a play. As you can understand, this tactic did not improve my popularity with my friends, who usually placed me in right field where I could do the least amount of damage. To their credit, my at least my friends allowed me to play, even though I was not the most valuable player.

As I recall these childhood memories, there are many disjointed images cycling in my brain. I remember that, for a long time, my brothers, sisters and I shared one raggedy bicycle. hen, about the time I was in sixth grade, my father saved up enough money to purchase four used bicycles from someone who had worked at Skidmore College. I cannot describe the joy, the feeling of freedom we had when we got these bikes, which allowed us to explore larger areas around our house. We were warned by our parents not to ride on road, and for the most part we heeded these warning for fear of retribution. However, we would ride for hours after school on trails that went through the woods near our home, leading us past swamps and other interesting spots. We always made sure we arrived home before our parents, who probably knew what we were up to but never said a word about it.

In the early summertime we took 5-gallon buckets and ventured into the fields to pick wild strawberries. As the summer would progress, we picked blackberries and blueberries that my mother and grandmother on my father's side would use to make sweet, delicious strawberry, blackberry and blueberry jelly. Grandma also would bake fruit pies and cobblers, the smell and taste of which remain etched in my brain even though the accident wiped out my senses of taste and smell.

We were outside a lot in those days. This is probably because we did not have television. One game I remember playing was "Wagon Train." We had our own little red wagon and we'd make it into a covered wagon, and pull ourselves around, pretending we were horses. We took turns playing the horses. Other children in the area would bring their wagons down to our house and we'd form a train and venture into the fields, pretending to explore the Wild West. We'd often pretend we were fighting Indians and bandits on our adventures.

While childish adventures bright us temporary rays of joy, spiritual exploration is what truly quenched my soul. I accepted Jesus Christ as my savior at the age of 12 while attending tent revival with my family in Glens Falls, NY. It was at that moment the Lord called me to join his ministry and spread the Gospel. At that time, in 1962, my family belonged to the Mount Olive Baptist Church in Saratoga Springs.

This was significant to me because my grandparents on my mother's side had been members of that congregation for many years. We were all active in the church, singing in the youth choir, participating in the Baptist Youth Fellowship, and serving as junior ushers.

Discourse among the congregation at Mount Olive over an issue that's been long forgotten caused my parents to leave that church and join First Baptist Church and its predominantly white congregation. Interestingly, Mount Olive and First Baptist were at opposite ends of College Street in Saratoga Springs. By this time, however, my religious fervor was only escalating and I was searching for ways to express the might and energy of the spirit that was in me. It's about that time I began exploring traditions of the Pentecostal church, and was intrigued by such traditions as baptism of the holy spirit, speaking in tongues and other open expressions of faith. It all seem so freeing to me, so I began attending Baptist services in the morning and Pentecostal services in the evening. I continued this bi-congregational practice through college.

About the time I accepted Jesus Christ as my savior, I began preaching. In fact, I spent many weekends between the ages 12 and 18 traveling throughout the state preaching at youth events sponsored by the American Baptist Convention.

My big mouth was finally being put to good use, and I'm sure my brothers and sisters enjoyed the reprieve. (I should add here that my discovery of faith enabled me to better endure my struggles in the classroom. It motivated me to work hard to get good grades, which I did, setting a platform for future academic excellence.)

As my faith grew, I began seeking out mentors, persons of God from whom I could learn the "tools of the trade," so to speak. I remember my piano teacher, Ruth Mallory, gushing one lesson about attending a weekend healing service in West Virginia presided over by evangelist Catherine Coolman.

Mrs. Mallory had only recently accepted Jesus Christ as her savior, and she spoke in glowing terms how this woman of God impacted her life. She told I could listen to Ms. Coolman was on the radio every night, a suggestion which spawned another activity that began habit for me.

So intrigued was I by what Mrs. Mallory said, I saved money to purchase a old transistor radio. I remember having to wedge a knife in the speaker to help with both reception and balance. Anyway, that radio opened up a world that I never knew existed. Each night, between 9 p.m. and 11 p.m., I could listen to preachers whom I soon came to consider my greatest mentors. They included Coolman, A.A. Allen, R.L. Shambauch, and the Rev. Ikewin Coater. You couldn't pull me away from the radio most evenings, as I absorbed their words, their styles and their ability to stand as a witness for Christ. I would continue doing this during my college years at Syracuse University. One weekend while I was in college, my mother agreed to join me on the almost 8-hour trip to New York City to see Shambauch and Rev. Coater in person. The excursion was not much of an inconvenience for my mother, as she was a huge fan of Rev. Coater. But I digress.

I would be remiss if I did not mention other spiritual mentors from my youth, including the Rev. Julius Larkins and the Rev. John L. Smith at Mount Olive, and the Rev. Roland Tingley at First Baptist Church.

My growing religious zeal was tempered by my parent's insistence that I get a college education, and earn a degree in something that could land me a "real" job. While I knew in my heart that I would someday be a minister, I respected my parent's wishes. I majored in speech communications and dramatic arts, and minored in urban studies at Syracuse, where I earned my bachelor's degree. Essentially, I was qualified to be a social worker, which is the kind of work I would do for a good portion of my early professional life. While at Syracuse, I attended St. Paul Baptist Church and St. Matthews Church of Christ, both in Utica. The Rev. Dr. Franklin Upthegrove, pastor of St.

Paul's, is another person of influence in my early preaching. While in college, I served as a "supply" preacher, meaning I filled in for pastors of various congregations in the area when they were out of town. This permitted me to keep in touch with my calling while pursuing a more practical academic path, at least according to my parents. On a side note: One year before I graduated from college I became a missionary for the Southern Baptist Mission.

Upon graduation in 1974, I remained in Albany and was hired working in the chronic care unit of county department of social services. I worked mostly with drug addicts and alcoholics suffering from severe psychological disorders. I also served as an assistant pastor of the Central Baptist Church there, a position I assumed after becoming a licensed minister.

In 1975, I moved to Kansas City, Mo., to attend the Midwest Baptist Theological Seminary to begin work on my master's degree in divinity. I planned to finally become an ordained minister, which was my heart's desire since I was 12. While in seminary, I served as a supply pastor for St. Luke United Methodist Church. The temporary move to work in the Methodist church as spawned by a desire of church officials to attract more African-Americans to that particular congregation. In my mind it only added to the rich texture of experiences I was gaining, which I believe would make me a better minister.

I put my master's degree and ordination on hold to answer a call by the Southern Baptist Convention to serve as a "church planter" in Peoria, Ill. Moving to Peoria in 1977, I oversaw the creation of Agape' Baptist Church to help fulfill a spiritual need in that area. (Agape' is a Greek word, meaning "unselfish" or "Godly" love.) I was ordained in 1978, and would remain in Peoria until 1985.

Personal life changes brought me to Columbus, Ohio in 1985, where I worked a variety of social service jobs while becoming active at Mount Olivet Baptist Church, where I was an associate minister. I re-energized my divinity studies by attending and earning a master's degree in 1990 from The Methodist School of Theology in Delaware, Ohio. My faith-calling prodded me further, and on May 20, 1995 I earned a doctoral degree in theology from the United Theological Seminary in Dayton, Ohio.

I worked as a manager for the Ohio Civilian Conservation Corps between 1995 and 2000. In 1992, I founded Adoration and Peace Baptist Church, which originally operated out of a chapel at an independent-living center for adults in Columbus. As our congregation grew, we began looking for our own building, finding one on the Near East Side of Columbus in 2003. Everything was going well; the pieces of my life seemed to be coming together. I was fulfilling my dream of being a pastor of my own church. Everything seemed so right that weekend when I left to attend the dedication of my grandson in Peoria.

Now I know God had other plans for me. ✝

Fence heartens minister

Byline: Delvin Harshaw, Cox News Service
Date: December 5, 2003
Publication: *Dayton Daily News* (OH)

SPRINGFIELD - The Rev. Johannes J. Christian rubbed his gloved hand along the newly installed protective fencing on the Plattsburg Road bridge over Interstate 70.

"It's like a Christmas present," he said. "It's like Christmas." Thursday was the first time the Columbus minister had been to the bridge in Harmony Twp. since nearly two years ago, when he was blinded by a 15year-old Harmony Twp. boy who threw a 7-pound rock from the overpass that crashed through Christian's windshield and hit him in his face.

"Thank God this is covered," the pastor of Adoration and Peace Baptist Church said of the bridge he walked using a cane and the arm of his friend, Vernon Malone. The fencing the Ohio Department of Transportation installed this week brought his ordeal to a conclusion, he said.

"I only wish it was covered that night. I still would be able to see," he said.

He and his 16-year-old foster son, Brian Renier, were returning home to Columbus after a christening ceremony for Christian's grandson in Peoria, Ill., on July 9, 2001, when the incident occurred. Renier reached over and brought the car to a stop.

Jacob C. McNary, then 15, confessed, explaining that the rock that hit Christian was the second he had thrown. McNary was sentenced to 12 years in prison for his guilty plea in adult court to attempted murder.

A lawsuit Christian filed against the boy's family in July 2002 for $25,000 in compensatory damages, plus punitive damages and attorneys fees, is pending in Clark County Common Pleas Court.

Christian has had nearly two years of reconstructive surgery, the last of the 30 operations occurring in November. The procedures are finished for now: "Unless they can find a way to restore my sight."

#

> "To open their eyes, and to turn them from darkness to light, and from the power of Satan unto God, that they may receive forgiveness of sins, and inheritance among them which are sanctified by faith that is in me."
>
> - Acts 26:18

Spiritual Warfare

The details of the incident became crystal clear to me during the court trial. Although I remained hospitalized during the initial proceedings, when Jacob McNary appeared before the Clark County (Ohio) Juvenile Court, members of my family and friends were there in force.

Returning to the hospital after going to court, they would let me know, in detail, how things went. It was during this time that I implored my brothers and sisters, my children, and my friends to make sure they represented God and represented Him well. I wrote notes stating:

"We are Christians both in name and faith. We must act like Christians. We must show them forgiveness. We must show them compassion. We must try to empathize with their pain, just as others are trying to feel and understand our pain."

The latter part of that directive became more obvious to me from the number of phone calls, cards and letters I received from across the country from other preachers and lay people from all walks of life, races and religions. People seemed to go out of their way to let me know that they felt my pain. Now, I know they could not sense my blindness, nor could they feel the actual physical pain in my head, but it became very apparent that my life had touched the lives of so many others. I heard from people who worked with me at the Ohio Civilian Conservation Corps, and from students and parents I helped train in that capacity. These were people who I considered acquaintances at best; I had never socialized with them, but they sought me out to share expressions of love, compassion and support.

After returning home after months of reconstructive surgery and rehabilitation, I listened to Clark County Prosecutor Steven A. Schumaker, who was preparing for trial after it as determined that Jacob McNary would be tried as an adult. Mr. Schumaker gave me a better understanding of exactly what happened the night of the accident. He shared with me vivid details about how Jacob and his two cousins spent that fateful evening. The boys met in Jacob's room and performed some sort of séance, for lack of a better word. I don't know what his room looked like, except by the description that I have been given. I'm told that in his room there were writings on the wall that represented those of gang violence, or gang warfare, or gang signs, or even, if you will, signs of devil worship. These symbols and signs could be seen only under a black light.

I was told that law enforcement officials learned it was not the first time this group of boys were out throwing rocks from that particular overpass, which was near Jacob's Harmony Township home. I remember praying that it would be their last such effort. Earlier that evening, Jacob expressed frustration over the fact that they had only hit the trailer of a passing tractor-trailer. Again, I thanked God they did not hit another windshield that day.

Mr. Schumaker continued sharing the details. I learned that Jacob attempted to agitate the others that were with him. He was so intent on hitting something, but better yet, hitting someone and cause bodily harm. His cousins testified that they urged Jacob to stop throwing rock, saying, "Let's get back to the house." But he persisted. He was on a mission. He was determined that he was out there to do something that, perhaps, he had never done before. So with each aim, it seems as though, he intended to hit a "bulls-eye," like some perverse game of darts. He wanted to do some kind of damage that would make a mark for his own life.

Because I really don't know what was going through his mind, I can only imagine that he had been dealing with a lot of personal problems, and these issues drove him to the bridge that night. Even though he's been questioned by countless other people, including prosecutors, the police, and several psychologists, I do not know that there has been a full explanation as to why he felt so intent on doing physical harm. All I can conceive is that this boy was severely tormented. Authorities know that he was loner, who had severe anti-social tendencies. Yet in court, he seemed very docile. By virtue of what he said in court and what the psychological exams revealed, he found it very difficult to express himself in words. The cadence and simplicity of his speech patterns revealed that his formal education had been interrupted on more than once occasion. Why, I wondered? Did he struggle in classes like I did? Did he have a learning disability that had gone untreated or undiagnosed? Could that happen today like it happened when I was young? Aren't we suppose to have more knowledge and resources to help challenged or troubled children like myself and Jacob? Did he get any support from his parents? What was his family life really like? I had problems in school, but I knew I was loved by my parents, and I knew they were determined to see me become successful in life. Did Jacob try to fill the various voids in his life by participating off-task, dangerous and criminal activities? Did he fill his time with things he believed productive, even though what seemed productive to him was really deemed destructive according to societal mores.

Why did the pleas of his cousins fall on deaf ears? Why did it only motivate him further down a dark corridor of activity? "Come on, Jacob, let's go back to the house," they said.

"Let's go back and do something else. You're going to hurt someone."

From my perspective, it was as if Satan himself was speaking through Jacob, when he turned and said, "I am not leaving yet. I am not done. I realize what might happen. Why do you think I'm out here? I'm on a mission."

I do not believe it was Jacob's intent to hurt me personally. I do not think that he really knew what he was doing; I think he was acting on instinct. Having stated that, I do believe that God knew in his infinite wisdom what was about to happen. I think Satan was in control at that point, and as a result, what Satan willed for my life came about through Jacob McNary.

I believe a confluence of demonic possession and divine will occurred when Jacob picked up that rock and tossed it over the side of that bridge. How do you explain the perfect timing with which this happened? Who would ever dream that a rock could land with such a significant force and accuracy to break the windshield and land perfectly on my face? I'm pretty sure bookmakers in Las Vegas would summarily refuse that action, as the odds are just too insurmountable. What I do know is that Jacob got his bulls-eye.

As I've stated, I remember hearing a crash, but nothing else after that. I do not remember the pain that I should have felt as my face exploded. I can only imagine that, as the rock hit my face, it sprung my seat into a reclining position. That is how I was told paramedics found me, bleeding profusely. My blood was splattering everywhere. My blood, the blood that God had given me had been freed from its mortal container, released to flow wherever it wanted to flow. I think about my foster son, Brian, who had to sit there and look at me. Imagine his horror? No wonder he believed me to be dead. I would have thought the same thing. All he could see was my blood everywhere he looked. It was even on his clothes.

It is amazing to me, when talking about details of the incident, how a 16 year old had the fortitude to grab the wheel, step over the center console, release the cruise control, put his feet on the gas and brake, and steer the car to the side of the road. I don't even understand how he could have done that with glass and blood all around him, and with no highways lights to guide him. And when you think that I was laying lifeless in the driver's seat as he did this, it's even more incredible. Now consider the contrasting behaviors of these two boys. Brian became an accidental player in Jacob's game, and I know it was God's will to put Brian in that time and place. God had a purpose for Brian, just as Satan had a purpose for Jacob. If Jacob was Satan's executioner, then Brian fulfilled God's providence by redeeming my life.

Jacob McNary and his cousins knew they hit something. It was only when they heard the squealing of brakes did they get on their bikes and return to Jacob's house. Did they call for help? No. Did they tell an adult, so help could be summoned? No. Jacob's cousins testified that, when they arrived back at the house, the they "clowned around" for a bit and went to sleep. They went to sleep hearing sirens in the distance. It wasn't until the next morning, after hearing about the accident on the headline news, that one of the boys told Jacob's mother about what happened previous night, confessing that they may be responsible for the accident.

The information I just shared about Jacob's part in my accident was revealed during court proceedings.

Other details, however, were not revealed until the day before a criminal trial was set to begin. Prosecutor's shared this information with my brother, Arthur, who in turn shared it with me. Information forwarded in the 11th hour was that the boys had indeed experimented with devil worship. They told prosecutor's that, beneath a rug in the middle of the floor in Jacob's bedroom, was a drawing of a pentagram. They said on occasion, they burned black candles placed at the corners of the pentagram to call up Satan.

The boys provided more details of their Satanic obsession, telling the prosecutor that the walls of Jacob's bedroom were painted white, but that transparent paint had been used to write the words, "Death," "Satan," and "Kill," which would only appear when illuminated with a black light. The prosecutor was overwhelmed that all of this information came forward just 10 minutes before the trial was to begin. He had no idea that it was spiritual warfare that they were up against.

I understand more today, than I did at the time, when I was using most of my mental and physical reserve to stay alive. Records from the Ohio Department of Transportation revealed that at least seven other "rock throwing" incidents at that bridge had occurred in the three years prior to my accident. We may never know for a fact whether Jacob and his cousins are responsible for these incidents, but it's apparent that it was not their first time they engaged in dangerous activities.

Jacob told psychologists that he was doing what he thought Satan wanted him to do. I believe God had predestined and preplanned my life, and that Jacob's actions had been preordained as well. My brother, Arthur, tells me that God wanted to do great works through me and Satan understands this. My brother believes that Satan tried everything in his power to destroy my life. Maybe? All I know is that I've talked to the doctors and they say it's beyond medical science that I am even alive today. They are amazed and they are overwhelmed. They do not even understand how a person could survive getting hit in the face with a 7-pound rock at 70 miles an hour. They simply do not have any answers. I contend that God has all the answers, and we need only ask the right questions to understand his will.

Who knows what divine power helped my family see through the pain to find compassion in their hearts for the McNary family. They actually had the strength and spiritual fortitude to embrace the McNary family when they first met them, saying, "We understand your hurt and pain. We just pray for your son, that he, too, might see the light."

Since the accident, my family and I have been approached by countless people who said that they weren't Christians before hearing about the accident, but are Christians now. They share how they never thought about spiritual warfare until after reading accounts of the accident and subsequent trial in the news media. I always tell them that I do not know for sure if Jacob was worshipping Satan, only that this is what he professed to authorities. I do know that God prevailed in saving my life so that I continue preaching his word. Just knowing there are people in the world like Jacob that Satan is working through is a stern and vivid reminder that we must always wear our armor of God. My family believes I was wearing a full armor of God, and that my foster son, Brian, had God's sword in his hand to be able to stop the car.

When I think about Satan having the ability to look through a peephole and devise plans to create life-altering catastrophes, I think about God and His greater plans. I think about how the Word of God in Jeremiah, which states, "Before you were born, I knew you while you were yet in your mother's womb." That scripture is really significant. "While you were yet in your mother's womb, I knew you." It helps me to understand that God has a strategic plan for all our lives, as he did for mine.

I remember shortly before the accident how it just seemed like my life was finally pulling together, that I finally had a purpose and direction. I was able to leave my job with the state and had purchased a little apartment building. I had been working day-in and day-out, repairing it so that I would be able to have a source of income from rents to supplement the income I made being a pastor of a small church. I remember how my preaching had taken a whole new slant. It was so powerful, and you could feel the weight of God's anointing in the messages. There was a young man in our church named Jeff Scott, and he was literally bringing people by vanloads on Sunday mornings. It seemed like I was on the way up, going somewhere and going somewhere rather quickly. In all honesty, I don't know where I was going, but I can see how God was in control of what was happening.

Maybe the transformations that were occurring in my life threatened Satan on some level, and he decided to wage an all out war against me and against what God was trying to do in and through me. Satan declared war on my life and my ministry. If anything, my accident has helped understand the connection between the spirit realm and the physical realm. Jacob's actions were spawned from Satan. He used a child who was dabbling in spiritual darkness to exact his perverse desires. I don't believe for one moment that Satan just meant to blind me. I don't believe for a second that he thought that he would just mangle my face. I believe that in spiritual warfare his ultimate aim was to kill and destroy me, to silence me and not allow me to preach the gospel. I think that it's easy for me to see the power of God display itself. When I say, "Greater is He that's in me than he that's in the world," I think I'm saying that God kind of looked at my life like He looked the life of Job, and said, "Satan, you can touch him, but you can't destroy him. You can tear him down, but you cannot tear him apart. You can hold him up, but you can't stop him."

Because of everything I have endured, there's more strength and more power in me now than ever before. I've gained not only the power to forgive, but through the power of forgiveness, I have gained a new strength and a new confidence in my own self. I've seen changes in the growth of my family, my friends, and I've even witnessed these changes in strangers. I'm encouraged to know that, through it all, God gets the glory. That night I received a gift of love and mercy from God, who spared my life and strengthened my resolve.

I can't explain how and why I am alive, but I am. I have been told that if the rock penetrated one inch deeper into my skull, my brain would have been crushed. If it had fallen two inches lower, I would have been decapitated. And if the rock struck my chest, it would have crushed my ribs into my heart and probably killed me instantly. Some may I am lucky, and in many ways I am. I consider myself fortunate to walk in the grace of God. Just as Satan calculated his moves to get the rock to land on my face, I know that God was just as calculating in knowing how far to allow that rock to fall in order to preserve my brain, my memories of the past, and the possibilities of my future.

God not only guided my life that night. He was also with Brian, my foster son.

Just as the moments of my life were preordained, so were Brian's. God knew that Brian would be placed in a foster home, and that the foster home be my home. God knew there would be a disruption in Brian's previous foster home, and that I would get the call asking me to take responsibility for this young man. All of this had happened months ahead of time. Again, my mind revisited the verse that said, "…Before I knew you, while you were yet in your mother's womb." The Word also states: "The steps of a righteous man are ordered by God."

Sometimes when harsh and unpleasant situations in our lives occur, we don't think of them as though our lives are being ordered by God. We don't think of our footsteps being ordered, but they really are. Is it possible for all of the events that had to transpire in my life and in Brian's life, and the lives of all the people that we have come into contact with, since our birth, to bring us to the very moment when that rock came through the window to be coincidental? That meant that every experience that Brian's mother ever had from the time that she conceived him, as well as every incident in my life since I was born, happened to put us in the same place at the same time. The concept is more than my mind can comprehend, and I don't know if I can even use words that can justify what actually happened, other than to say that I know that God knew what was happening. Please understand. I am not saying that God is responsible. I am merely pointing out the predestined part of our lives, including the spiritual contracts that we have with one another.

Even in the days and weeks after the accident, my brother, Arthur, and I would share many spiritual contracts. For example, he drove me back and forth to the hospital, and would literally carry me on his back when I was too weak to walk. He felt my pain and suffering in ways no one else could understand unless they walked in his shoes. I also shared spiritual contracts with my children. Prior to the accident, I had carried them for 12, 23, 26 and even 28 years of their lives. Now they would have to carry me, a thought with just blows my mind. As a parent, I've become comfortable in the care-giving role. At my age, I did not expect that our roles would be exchanged so soon. They are concerned about my daily needs, my physical needs, and even my spiritual needs. I love them and am grateful that God has blessed me with so many brothers and sisters in Christ, with whom I share these spiritual contracts.

The more I think about it, the more I see God's hand in the situation, as well as the spiritual contracts that I have had with people throughout my life. I realize that the contracts go deeper. The spiritual relationships go deeper. How ironic it was that my plastic surgeon, Dr. Steven Schmidt, is a Man of God, who sees his ministry as the restoration of the human body. He worked over me as if his duties were under a personal contract with God; a contract willing him to repair God's vessel so that I could be back in the pulpit, preaching and doing the will of God. How unique God is in creating his people. Through the skilled hands of the Dr. Schmidt, God literally repaired every bone in my head. I described my face as having been taken off, or not having a face. During my recuperation, my children referred to me as "The man without a face." Yet, with wire mesh and bones, and with the skilled hands of a man of God, the same face that God created has been recreated. The image that God created was once again visible in the eyes of man. ☦

(Author's note: This article is an edited version of one that ran on the front page of the Dayton Daily News on March 27, 2005.)

The power of Forgiveness

Four years after a teenager's actions stole his sight and nearly his life, a minister reaches out to his assailant and finds strength in God

By Khalid Moss

His mouth was sore and he wasn't feeling well. Considering he's undergone 30 facial surgeries in four years, it wasn't hard to understand his discomfort But when the subject of forgiveness came up, the **Rev. Johannes J. Christian,** pastor of Adoration and Peace Baptist Church in Columbus, pushed aside the pain and spoke about one of his favorite subjects: The power of prayer.

Forgiveness and prayer are something Christian knows a lot about. On this Easter Sunday, they're something he'll have reason to contemplate.

On the evening of July 9, 2001, as he and his foster son were driving back to Columbus on Interstate 70, a (7-pound) rock flew over the Plattsburg Road overpass in Clark County. The rock—hurled by a

15-year-old Harmony Twp. Boy—burst through the windshield of Christian's car and smashed into his face.

The result: horrific damage to his head, nose, mouth and throat. The loss of his sight.

One of the physicians treating Christian that awful night was Dr. Stephen Schmidt, a Dayton plastic surgeon who happened to have strong Christian values.

"Johannes basically broke every bone in his face from the top of his skull to the bottom of his lower jaw," Schmidt said. "There was a hole where his eyes were suppose to be that I could put my fist into.

"Considering his injuries, which were life-threatening at the time, he functions pretty well today. He's still blind, but he can smell and I taste. He preaches every Sunday and has joined me in mission work to Belize and Guatemala. He's able to do almost everything he used to do."

In the weeks following the rock-throwing incident, the doctor/ patient relationship between Schmidt and Christian blossomed into a shared faith walk that, Christian said, has been blessed for both men.

"We've developed a wonderful relationship," Christian said. "He's a really fantastic Christian man. We pray together before surgeries and we've grown to love and respect each other."

There was, however, another far more difficult relationship that found its way through the midst of Christian's pain.

It was between the injured preacher and Jacob McNary—the juvenile who threw the rock, was convicted of attempted murder and is now serving a 12-year sentence for the crime at Madison Correctional Institute in London, not far from where it happened.

Months after the incident, Christian received several letters and an Easter card from McNary.

"He asked for my forgiveness and tried to apologize in a very feeble way," Christian recalled. "In one letter he said he wished he was dead. That's when I wrote him back and said, 'Let me help you. If I can forgive you, you can forgive yourself.

Christian admits the seed of forgiveness took a while to germinate

"When I was in the hospital, the Lord kept reminding me of his prayer: 'Give us this day our daily bread and forgive our trespasses as we forgive those who trespass against us.' It kept ringing in my ear.

"Finally, the Lord spoke to me and said, 'Johannes, remember the time you stole candy from the store when you were little? I forgave you for that.' My thought was, 'Hey, don't you guys forget anything up there? Soon after, the Lord moved on my heart and I began the process of forgiving," Christian said.

Mc Nary couldn't be interviewed for this story, but Jim Chamberlin, a retired Springfield school teacher and GED counselor for the Clark County jail, has tutored the young inmate and continues to be his partner in faith.

"The first time I saw that young criminal in his cell, I was struck by this handsome, boyish freshman who seemed so very young, small and vulnerable," Chamberlin said. "When he told me what he had done, he shook his head incredulously as if unable to fully comprehend it himself. Then he said, 'The fellow I almost killed said he is praying for me that I might become a

Christian.'

"Being a long-time Christian myself, I asked Jacob if he wished to be saved. His response was, 'Yes."

Chamberlin said McNary, now 18, wants to become a Christian songwriter so he can warn kids not to make the same mistakes he made.

"He wants to help other young people learn about Jesus and to keep them from going to hell. Jacob tells me that he reads his Bible constantly and is trying to maintain a Christian lifestyle under very difficult circumstances," Chamberlin said.

As he approached this Easter season, his fourth since the violent act that blinded him, the minister is reflective—philosophical even— about the ways in which a higher power made its presence felt through the whole terrible thing. "God could have stopped that rock from coming through the window," Christian said "But he elected no to.

"The incident has made me a much stronger individual. I am not the same person I was four years ago. This thing has raised my visibility as a person, a preacher and as a spokesman for victims everywhere."

I was a good man then, but God has really tried to make be better."

####

> "But he that shall blaspheme against the Holy Ghost hath never forgiveness, but is in danger of eternal damnation."
>
> - Mark 3:29

"Okay, God, Take Me."

I was in a cell of darkness, trapped in a cage of pain, sorrow and rage that consumed me as I lay in a hospital bed once I began to comprehend what really happened to me. It hit me that I was no longer going to be in control of my life in the sense I was before the accident. I would need to depend on others until the day I died, and the blunt force of that realization hit me harder than the rock Jacob McNary tossed over a bridge.

I spoke, well, rather I argued with God, desperately trying to make sense of the senseless, to find reason in the incomprehensible, and a purpose for circumstances that placed me in this hospital bed looking like something from science experiment gone horribly wrong:

I was tired of the pain and the torment, and I just knew the easiest thing for me to do would be to die. After all, I wasn't that far from death. It couldn't be that hard to stop breathing and just go on home to glory, or to wherever I might be ending up. I remember closing my eyes and saying, "Okay, God, take me. I'm dead now. I'm not living. I'm not going to breath." At one point I could feel my own spirit leaving my body. I thought I was floating to heaven, on my way there. At last, I would be at peace. I wouldn't have to deal with forgiving anyone. I wouldn't have to deal with being blind or any of the other things that were wrong with me. I could just die.

Suddenly, I was in heaven. I don't know whether this was a dream, whether I was living it, or even if it was for real, but it seemed so real to me. It seemed like when I got to heaven, God said, 'No, not now.' He said, 'Go on back.' It seemed like this happened more than once, maybe twice. I don't remember whether there was a bright light, or a tunnel, or whether I was floating. I don't recall if somebody was carrying me away. All I know is that I had this very real feeling that I had died and gone to heaven. I felt like it was all over and I didn't have to deal with it no more.

Then the next thing I knew, I was still laying in the bed, hearing them say, "Deal with it," "not now," or "come back." How could it be different? And why were you asking me to do something that so many other people around me couldn't seem to do? It wasn't a lesson for somebody else. It was a lesson for me. I began to think how grateful I needed to be that God forgave me for all of the dastardly deeds that I had done; about my own salvation experience and how sorry I was for my sins, how I asked God to cleanse me, and He said he did.

Oh, I'm not trying to preach a sermon. I'm trying to drive home a point. And then the point I'm trying to drive home is one that we all have to forgive. And there are many faces, not just mine. Many reasons that we have to forgive others, many things we need to forgive them for. This time it was God speaking to me.

Why do people hurt other people? How do we live in it so easily? Television makes it look so easy. You take a gun, you point it at someone, you shoot them, and they fall down. They die. There's no pain. There's not really a whole lot of blood. What went through that young boy's mind when he threw the rock? He couldn't have thought very much of his life or the life of anyone else for that matter, especially my life.

My mind was going in a different direction now. It wasn't so much forgiving as it was trying to examine what I was supposed to be forgiving. I realized that when people hurt someone, that it's just a way of showing that they really don't care about the value of another person's life. For some reason we seem to think that life really isn't worth very much. We act as though other people aren't important, that they don't count for very much, that their value isn't something that's readily thought of. Somehow we discount them and we make believe that they don't exist. Sometimes it seem we truly believe we are greater than that other person, but in reality we really don't think very much of ourselves. So perhaps when we're hurting others, we really are doing unto them what we would do unto ourselves? What else can it be? To think that someone's life was worth so little that we could just cancel it out. Isn't that what happens every time there's a drive-by-shooting? How senseless they are. We kill people over a blunt, or over a nickel bag, or over what someone owes us for a kilo. We kill. We kill somebody because they had an affair with your husband or wife, or girlfriend or boyfriend. We think their life isn't worth very much. We kill somebody because we're angry or we're mad. We kill somebody. Every time I listen to the radio I hear about somebody being killed. There are times that whole families are killed.

Just recently, a man killed his wife, his two children, then turned the gun and killed himself. Isn't it ironic that we think that life is so worthless that we can just rub each other out? I wouldn't begin to capitalize on the experience of what happened in Columbine, Colo. just a few years or months ago. That's what killing seems like sometimes. There's too much rage. There's so much rage inside of people that they're reaching out, lashing out and hurting others. I thank God my accident occurred before Sept. 11, 2001. I guess I always knew hate was global, but that just proved it. I lay here in the darkness that consumes me, dwelling on my ability to forgive while trying to understand why people do what they do.

We put classifications on hate. The rapist doesn't care about the other person. He, or she, is trying to meet a perverse need, a physical and emotional drive for power over another because of some deficiency in their own life. The child abuser is trying to work out his personal failures and psychological misgivings. The armed robber kills to take from another to quench a personal void. People are injured or killed for a plethora of reasons. The reasons merely serve to invalidate the lives of others. It seems no one has value. No one has purpose. No one believes life is a precious gift from God.

But we're talking about the life of men and women. And I keep thinking about the scripture, "And what is man that Thou are mindful of him, that Thou had made him just a little lower than the angels and the Son of Man that Thou hath visited him?" Breathe the breath of life into him when he said that. God said that.

Oh people, to realize that life is worth it. If you're willing to kill somebody, then you're saying that they're not somebody. What is recognizing what somebody else is worth have to do with our own healing? It's beginning to feel like I'm stuck and I can't move on with my own healing because I'm stuck on trying to figure out what this young man did to me. I'm beginning to feel that there's a correlation that unless I can reach out and help to understand who he is and where he is, that I can't move on from where I am.

Will that get my eyesight back? Will I get my nose back if I forgive him? If I forgive him, will I get a mouth back? Is that the reason I forgive him? Boy, that'd be easy. I'd forgive him if he'd give me my eyes. I'd forgive him a whole bunch, God, if you give me my nose. God, if you give me back my tongue and allow me to talk, then I could forgive him for everything. I could take back the thoughts about wanting to hit him with a rock. I could take back the thought of even being mad at you God, if you would heal me. I could forgive the world, if that meant I would be whole again, and not have to go through the pain and lay in this bed another day. Oh, God, if you'd reach down and just make a great miracle. Let a great light shine around this room and everything would be wonderful again. Wow, God, it would be so easy for me to forgive. I can forgive him. Oh, come on, Jesus, with your mighty miracle act, you allowed Peter to walk on water. You came through the clouds. You had the angels busting up at your birth. If that's what it takes God, I can forgive right now. I'm laying here, God, I forgive them. I can say I forgive them, God. Oh, I'm not bartering with you. I'm not making a deal … it's just … if that's what you wanted me to say, "I forgive him." OK, I forgive him. His life is worth a whole lot. His life in fact is worth 10,000 million dollars. I forgive him if you give me back my sight.

They're chattering. I hear angel wings fluttering around in here. No great divine intervention. You wanted me to say I forgave him. I said it. Life's worth more than the action of the people have taken against us. Even hanging on the cross, Jesus said, "Father, forgive them for they know not what they do." I get that. He was saying, "I'm the Son of God. I am God. I came down to earth and made myself a man, and I walked among them and they didn't even know who I was. Even as I hang on the cross, they don't know what they're doing. They don't know that they're killing the Son of Man."

We call ourselves Christians, which mean we are Christ-like. It's lonely in this room and I got my head hung down now because I realize I've been ranting and raving, and sitting and crying, and screaming on the inside like nobody's ever been hurt like I've been hurt. But Jesus is saying, "I was hurt and I was bruised." He says that I want him to figure out this thing called forgiveness.

I'm trying to work with it here, but I guess I need your help to find it because I really need you to help me with this. I've got to forgive. I'm really trying to forgive this guy, a kid who reportedly worshipped the devil. He didn't know I was a preacher. He didn't know I was even a man of God. All he knew was it was a car. Is this true, God?

This is so freaky. It's like I'm dreaming. It's like somebody's telling me look deeper. Look at it; grapple with it; wrestle with it. I am wrestling.

Look at the spirituality. You always tell people about the spirit realm and the human realm go hand-in-hand. Look at it. You preached that sermon about the balance between the Spirit and man. Look at it in that term. Look at it. The Spirit was dealing with that young man. The Spirit was pulling at him, was taunting him. He was a worshipper of darkness. He was under the rule of Satan. Satan was using him. He was just a vessel. He didn't know what he was doing, did he? He was just doing a deed. He knew no more than just a bottle carrying some water from one spot to another. It wasn't him. It was Satan and his imps. Don't you understand? The whole reason wasn't that boy. The reason wasn't him. The reason wasn't to put your eyes out. The whole reason was Satan wanted to kill you, to silent you. He used someone else. He used a boy. He twisted his mind and he said that life wasn't worth living. His life wasn't worth much, so no one else's life was worth much.

God is talking to me. He's telling that the boy hurt so much on the inside it didn't matter. "He's so mixed up it didn't matter. You don't have to know him to know that. Look at the deed. He knew who was in the car. Satan knew how fast the car was going and what speed the rock had to fall at, and how quickly it needed to hit. He knew how to hit your face. Don't you see or understand? You're so busy being caught up in the pain. So busy being caught up in sightlessness. You used to sing that song, 'Lord, let me be. I want to be a follower of Christ.' He didn't know who you were but Satan wrote a big "DIE" on his wall that could be seen with a black light. Think about it."

Understand rage. I'm told that the people that bombed the World Trade Center were on spiritual missions. All they knew was they were flying planes, but they didn't even know that they were flying planes to kill themselves and other people. So I was told they were just on missions. What brings people to kill like that? It can't be because people value life, but when you don't value life, it's like—Bam!

God's back now: "Then I want you to grapple with it. I don't know what it is. Is beating that guy going to make it more bearable for you to not have a face? No. You must bear it on the cross."

This thing haunts me. If I forgive him, it's not for eyesight, it's not for a nose. It's for the value of his life, because he's so convenient in my heart. I want it to be so other people can see it, and feel it and if I forgive him. It was easy to say from the cross, "Forgive them for they know not what they do," but it was hard for someone who had the power to come down from the cross to hang there. And, yet, as a human he hung there and he bled, and he took the punishment, and he paid the supreme sacrifice. That's the hard part.

Are you telling me I must hang on a cross, God?

"Follow me," he replies. "Forgiveness is part of the cross. Only it's a need. It's an act. They shouldn't be self-centered and say, 'Oh, just as long as I deal with this thing about forgiving him, what if nothing happened?'

If I'd forgive him, it'd be that easy, you'd just let me die and go on to heaven.

"No, I don't think it's that easy. I don't see how that's going to happen. Forgive him."

It's crazy talking to myself like this.

"Now you don't question whether or not you really forgive him?" God retorts to me. "You must dig deep."

I don't know if I have the reserves to get me through? He just about knocked everything in me out.

"Never mind feeling sorry for yourself. Dig deep. Dig deeper. If you're going to forgive him, forgive him all the way. If you can't convince yourself you forgive him, you can't hope to convince your children to forgive him. You won't begin to convince the rest of the world that you've forgiven him. You've got to dig deep. Deeper, deeper, deeper; your debts were deep. I had to dig deep for you.

"That's the good thing about praying. Nobody knows what goes on inside your mind. This is just between you and me. And after all, I am

God. If you want to forgive him, then you got to forgive him. You got to convince yourself and you've got to convince me that you've forgiven him. And remember, I know it all. I know when you're joshing me, or I know when you're lying, and I know when you're for real. You must forgive him.

"Well, I'm coming down from glory, Christian, and if you're going to 'talk the talk' it's time to 'walk the walk.' You've been preaching forgiveness all these years now. I forgave you, now it's your turn. From where you are, I think you better look like forgiving him."

Does that mean that you want me to pray that he becomes a preacher, I said?

"No, just pray that he'll love me, and even if he doesn't change that I forgive him. I really forgive him," God said.

So if hitting me got him his bulls-eye, I bet he did a back flip and thought it was funny.

"Well, regardless of what he thought, I know the whole world is coming down on him right now. With people running around and saying that, he doesn't need you to say it too."

Oh God, I've totally lost my mind.

"Do you care what others think or do you care what I think?"

I really care what you think.

"Well, let's cut the comedy act and not worry about what other people are thinking. Like me, what I want from you is total surrender. What I want from you is total forgiveness. What I want for you is compassion for him, caring for him, feeling for him."

But isn't he Satan?

"No, he just thinks he belongs to Satan."

I've been holy on the outside, I guess I need to be holy on the inside.

At this point, whether I was still praying or dreaming, my healing pivoted on my ability to forgive Jacob McNary. My total healing, my emotional healing, my being made whole was all in him. It was all in my ability to forgive him. I was learning that it wasn't me that was doing the forgiving. It was Christ forgiving me, forgiving through me.

The more I prayed for him, the better I began to feel. The more I said, "To God be the glory, for God to reap the glory," the better I began to feel. It was in my forgiveness. As I reached out of myself and touched and tried to reach that young man, and as the angels came and lifted me and held me in the presence of God. But he didn't allow me to think about my eyesight, or my nose, or my mouth, or my pain. All I could think about was that young man and the value of his life. ☩

(Copy of the first letter Rev. Christian wrote to Jacob McNary in prison.)

Reverend Dr. Johannes J. Christian
691 Lilley Avenue
Columbus, Ohio 43205

September 23, 2002

Dear Jacob,

I hope that this letter finds you in the best of health. I continue to remember you in my prayers. I hope that you are still growing in the faith I am confident that God will give you the strength to make it through each coming day.

My prayers are also with your parents, as they move through this legal process.

I thank God that I am getting stronger as time passes along. I know that it is the grace of God that is helping me to adjust to my new life circumstances hope that you will remember me in your prayers. I will close now.

May God be with you,

Dr. Johannes J. Christian

> "... And forgive us our trespasses as we forgive those who trespass against us."
>
> *- Matthew 6:12*

Finding Forgiveness

While teetering between life and death, I received a message from God, through his Word, that pierced my soul and fueled a power within me forgive Jacob McNary for what he had done to me.

In the Bible, in Matthew the 6th Chapter, Jesus Christ speaks to his disciples in what is known as The Lord's Prayer. There's a portion where He says, "...And forgive us our trespasses as we forgive those who trespass against us." Forgive? Forgive whom? Forgive what? What does that mean? What was God requiring of his disciples? What does it mean in relationship to His Word where He says, "All have sinned and fallen short of the glory of God?" He forgave the sins of the world.

I laid in the hospital bed somewhere between consciousness and unconsciousness and tried to deal with what had happened to me. Internally, I thought I had dealt with the issue of forgiveness. I looked up the word, "Forgive." It means to give up the wish to punish or get even with; not to have hard feelings at or towards someone; to pardon or to excuse. Excuse means to forgive a debt. The act of forgiveness is to pardon

As I continued to grapple with the word forgiveness, in relationship to my Christian experience and my history of preaching, I realized that prayer then, was a plea for forgiveness that would otherwise remain unuttered. Our plea is constantly that Christ would forgive us. That God would forgive us and place us in a relationship with him that had no barriers. We assume that the blood of Christ transcends all of our iniquities, all of our unrighteousness and places us in a state where God does not recognize the wrong that we've done. Isn't a part of being Christian an innate willingness to forgive? It was as though Christ was expecting individuals to display their unselfishness through acts of forgiving others who are behaving unselfishly. Forgetting oneself to place others first is an unselfish act. The more I thought about it, the greater my understanding of forgiveness became. It wasn't just for me. It wasn't just for a few individuals. It was a challenge that God was giving to all of mankind. It was a challenge that was greater than our hurt, our pain, and our sorrow. It was a challenge that extended far beyond ourselves and that allowed others to see that we thought more of them or as much of them as we thought of ourselves. What a noble and Christ-like challenge it was. He was giving mankind the chance to reflect the same attitude he reflects as he forgives us our shortcomings, and even our intentional deeds.

As I grappled with the understanding of forgiveness I could see that it went way beyond my present situation. In our society, we live among so many horrific and devastating activities, activities that occur with increasing frequency that they seem almost mundane, almost trite.

However, these traumatizing events further intensify the complexity of this necessary act called forgiveness. Because of the times we are facing, there is such a great need for people to learn how to forgive. We, as Christians, must do it.

I thought about the child who had been molested and sexually abused. Was there an expectation that she would forgive the perpetrator? What about the child who had been abused physically, shaken, beaten, maimed or mangled? What about the bed wetter whose punishment was to have their feet placed boiling water, or they were made to sit on a pot filled with scalding hot water? What about the child who was burned with cigarette butts? What about those who were neglected or those that grew up with parents who had drug or alcohol addictions? Was there a need for them to forgive? What about the young girl who lost her virginity due to incest or because of some unspeakable deed performed by a family friend or neighbor? Did God expect her to forgive as well? My thoughts continued. What about the woman who was hauled into the back of a van and was molested or raped, perhaps at knifepoint or gunpoint? What about those women who, because of some prank or some perverted initiation right, are gang-raped? Does God expect them to forgive as well?

Oh, this thing of forgiveness, it's overpowering me. It's greater than I am. It's unending. What about those who robbed a bank? What about those who were hi-jacked in a plane? What about those whose house was burned up by an arsonist? What about those who were offended in some way? What about those who are neglected or forgotten in nursing homes? Was God expecting them to forgive as well? His act of kindness, his act of unselfishness, it goes far beyond what I could imagine. In fact, it was greater than me. It overwhelmed me.

I thought about all the times in life when we were hurt or when, in some way, the actions of others afflicted us or impacted us. Were there times when not showing forgiveness would be acceptable? When someone shoots your loved one, was that something that didn't need to be forgiven? Were there exceptions to the rule? There has to be. Don't people bend rules all the time without fear of retribution? I stretched my mind to try to figure out what could possibly be a thing that we would not have to forgive. Then I thought about how we taught children to say, "I'm sorry," and to wait for a response or indication from the other child that would say, "I accept your apology." This was an act of forgiveness. I could not remember during my own childhood, a time when my mother said that I didn't need to forgive. I could not remember any examples where Christ said it was acceptable to not forgive. What about those who were going through a divorce, and stooping to angry, nasty, and unchristian like levels to settle custody and property battles? Does this warrant forgiveness? Surely there must be an instance where it is acceptable for someone not to forgive. Yet that verse that goes back to the prayer he taught his disciples that simply says, "… And forgive us our trespasses as we forgive those who trespass against us." Is it this easy?

It was like there was a link between him forgiving us and us forgiving those who need to be forgiven by us.

Why would he link up my forgiveness with my ability to forgive another? What was I to gain by forgiving or by being forgiven? What was I going to get out of the act of forgiving? What would anybody gain by forgiving? What would be the sense in it? My mind kept racing on and on with these words of "Forgiving" and "Unselfish actions." Has happened to me happened to anyone else? Will the pain and my blindness go away if I just forgive? Was God somehow saying that when we forgave, we would not hurt anymore? Would it speed up the healing process and dull the pain? Am I experiencing a psychological deficiency, something that perhaps a psychologist or psychiatrist would have to deal with? Am I just having a problem psyching myself out? I don't know if my mind can comprehend it or if I am even bright enough to make it really happen? I am a pastor. How would I help somebody else in the future, if I really cannot help myself now?

I thought about the fact that I'd been preaching for almost 30 years. How many times have I said "The Lord's Prayer?" I thought about how many times I've said it before the congregation and told them that we needed to forgive others, as we wanted Christ to forgive us. I thought I meant it earnestly. I had good intentions, but now, I couldn't be so sure. I thought the biggest hurdles of my life were behind me. But now I was faced with a problem that was greater than me, and I could understand the perspectives of those around me who were hurt or still grieved from something that happened to them, yet they were being called upon to forgive. I was being called to forgive, but I realized that forgiving did not mean forgetting. A rape victim never forgets the fact that they were raped, neither does a child that was neglected or abused. Someone who is strung out on drugs probably never forgets the first time he lit up, or the experience of being hooked on the drug.

I do not think that there was an equation between forgiving and forgetting. However, somehow, I think that we would have to become over comers. But what did we gain by this act of forgiveness? It had to be a root, but what would it grow or produce for me? There had to be a reason, an explanation for it necessity. My mind hastened to try and process the lesson I believed God was teaching me, "What will you gain from forgiveness?"

I thought about the many people that I have counseled over the years. I remembered the John and Jane Does that I had helped through foster care. I remember the young man who used to come to my house in crisis because the Children Services agency had removed him from his home because they felt that his home was an unsafe place for him to be. I can remember, in prayer and in conversation, helping some of these young children to understand that, "No, mommy was not a bad person and she didn't mean to neglect them in such a way that they would have to be taken from their home." As time went on, I remembered trying to help them figure out how they could love their mommy after she didn't show up for the scheduled visit arranged by the agency. Even though they were devastated, I tried to help them understand that Mommy's behavior was not indicative of her true feelings toward them. While riding home in the car I would try to comfort them and at the same time tell them, "It's alright that you feel bad, but let's not hate Mommy because she didn't show up, because we are not quite sure why she couldn't come. Sometimes, even after knowing what happened, whether they just forgot or whether it wasn't important enough to them to show up, I, as a foster parent and Christian, still had to help that young person come to grips with what it meant to forgive.

One of my most sensitive encounters with counseling in forgiveness concerned a young rape victim, who sought help for the many problems she was trying to work through. She was sitting across from me at my desk, shivering and shaking as she recalled the tormenting details of how it felt to be violated in such a way. She was with me because she wanted to push ahead with their life. She wanted to move on from that dark place that consumed her. She wanted somehow to forget that act that had happened to her, but she was stuck. She was so stuck that she couldn't move. She trembled at the thought, of the mental images as she remembered the crime. I remember this young girl telling me every time she saw a man in blue jeans, it made her want to run and hide. It brought tears to her eyes because the perpetrator, the one who violated her, was wearing a pair of blue jeans with tattered ends on the cuffs. That is all she could remember about him, but what she could see, she couldn't forget. It was so hard for her because it hurt her so deeply.

God presented me with the opportunity to help her to learn how to forgive that man. However, in my own mind I wanted to take a bat and go up against the side of his head with it, smashing his head in and making him hurt the way that he had made the young girl hurt. There wasn't anything about me that wanted to be forgiving toward him, as I sat in that chair listening to her, seeing the pain and the unforgettable fear painted across her face. Yet, I kept telling myself that I had to help. I had to help her not only deal with what happened, but I also needed to show her that in relinquishing the debt that man had committed against her, she would be able to move forward and away from this bad place. I needed to tell her that she had to rise up over the action that had happened. How easy that was for me. I wasn't a rape victim. At least she didn't know whether I was a rape victim or not. So, I could preach the necessity of forgiveness, but how was I supposed to help her realize that she would gain some strength in the process. Was there some strength to be gained? What were the strengths? Oh, let me count them. I explained to her, "If you can learn to forgive that individual, you can regain forgiveness for wrongful deeds that you have done, as well as gain physical and emotional strength. Look to God as an example when forgiving others. Observe His perfection in forgiving, in His ability to forgive us."

A blind eye could see that if you could forgive someone else, then perhaps your healing process could move along quicker. I thought about it in my case. If it could take away the pain and speed up the healing process, then I could forgive him. The young man who had thrown the rock through my window had the same name that I had. My middle name was Jacob and his first name was Jacob. I could forgive him. Now I needed to forgive everyone else. I had to figure out how to forgive God because I was so angry. I was angry not only with the boy, but also at God. I was angry at the world. I was angry with the police for not being there. I was angry with the people that built the bridge, because there wasn't a cover over it even though other incidences like this had occurred. I was angry at the fact that nobody was out there to stop them. I was angry with the people that raised the young boy. I was angry with the school because they must have failed him. I was angry with his mother and his father. I was angry at everything around me. I was angry with the doctors and nurses because they couldn't get me back together again. They didn't make me well quick enough. I was angry. I was so angry one day, I woke up and tried pulling apart my face, trying to pull out the tubes, trying to pull out everything that was in me.

Oh, such anger. Oh, that not unforgiving spirit. All that energy that I expended, and it accomplished nothing. God was still sovereign. He still knew what I had gone through. It didn't seem to move God that I was mad. The police didn't know that I was mad at them. Jacob's mother and father, they didn't know I was mad at them. I doubt that Jacob knew that I was mad. What difference did it make if his name was the same as mine? I thought that was the most horrible thing of all! I thought about how good I had been. I thought I had been a great person. After all, I have loved young people. I'd loved my own children. I had thought that I was basically a good person. I tried to do "good" everywhere I went. After all, I was a man of God. I was a preacher. I'm not saying in any way that I was perfect, but I sure tried to help everybody. I had raised not only my four children, but I had raised more than 40 other children that had come to my home through foster care. I provided food, shelter, clothing, love and guidance to all these children. I taught them and trained them. I took them back and forth to school, to basketball practice, to dances, to roller skating rinks, and to picnics. I made sure they had visits with their parents and with their siblings. I went far beyond my duties, taking them on trips and vacations with me. I just knew I was a good person, and I just couldn't understand why this thing could be happening to me?

It didn't have anything to do with my goodness. It didn't have anything to do with my greatness. I knew Senators. I knew people in the House of Representatives. I'd met the Governor and his wife. If I call Columbus Mayor Michael Coleman, he'll take the call himself. The President of the United States received my last book and he sent me a card in response. I knew I was somebody and yet I just could not imagine how something so devastating and so horrible could happen to someone as good as me. I thought about many things that I had done, many of the good things. At times, I stood in the checkout line, in the grocery store and saw a mother with children, struggling to pay the bill. I also remembered the times when I reached out and said to the cashier, "Allow me to pay for her groceries." Reluctantly when she would ask what was my name, I'd simply say, "I'm just a friend of God. You go on." I remember one time, when a little boy was standing in front of me badgering his mother, "Oh, please let me have it." Mommy said, "No, we can't afford it." I remember asking her, "Would he read it if he had it?" "Oh, yes, he loves to read," she responded and asked the cashier how much was the total. I reached in my pocket for the two dollars, the cost of the magazine, telling him to go ahead and take it. I've done all these wonderful things. Yet, I laid in the hospital bed and could hear my children and those around me, but I was forced to communicate by writing on a piece of paper. I wasn't sure if they could read what I was writing. I realized how much that insignificant rock had changed my life in an instant.

At the hospital, people would tell me what had happened and how they found me, soaking in my own blood and appearing lifeless. They told me how someone had thrown a rock down over a bridge and it had gone through the windshield of my car, hurting my family and I. Every time I would doze off to sleep, I'd hear that words, "And forgive those our debts as we forgive our debtors." Through yet another surgery, every time I would drift off, I'd hear those words. How could I forgive him? I didn't know what this kid looked like. I didn't know where he lived. I didn't know where he came from. The more I heard about him, the more I got confused, angry, and reluctant to forgive. It wasn't bad enough that they told me he knew he could hurt someone by dropping rocks, but there were others with him who pleaded with him to stop. I was told that he said it really didn't matter to him if he hurt someone or not. After all, that's what he was trying to do. He was out there wanting to hurt someone. Well, if he wanted to hurt someone, did I still have to forgive him? I was the last component to the completion of his mission. I now had the scars and the cane to prove it. Did I have to forgive him? When he wanted to do bad to somebody, did I have to forgive him? Even if he didn't know that I would be in the car that night, did I still have to forgive him?

My, God, it just hurt so much! The pain was there. The doctors were pulling at me. The nurses were yanking me around, and yet my mind was saying, "Forgive. Forgive." I wrote on my paper, telling my children, "We need to forgive, my children."

"Yeah, daddy, we need to forgive. Right. Whatever." I couldn't talk but I wrote, "No, no, no, that's not the attitude. That's not what God expects of us." Oh, I could write it but God knows I didn't believe it. I felt like somebody else would have to forgive Jacob and his cousins. It really couldn't be me. How could I forgive him? It was too much to handle. I couldn't see my daughter's faces. I couldn't even say a word to them through my mouth and yet I'm struggling with this act of forgiveness.

I was struggling to deal with all of these changes in my life, and now I am supposed to forgive. Then I overheard someone say that Jacob was Caucasian. That didn't matter because I did not know how to forgive him anyway. Then I heard the words of a long-forgotten song ringing in my head, "I never promised you a rose garden." Oh, God, I did not know the cross would be that heavy. I didn't know the cross would mean I would have to forgive someone for smashing in my face, taking off my nose, plucking out my eyes, and taking away my ability to speak. I couldn't believe God would expect that of me. After all, I'd been a great man. I'd preached to hundreds and thousands of people around the country. After all, I was a doctor. I had a

Doctorate of Ministry. I was a symbol of leadership. I was somebody to reckon with in the community. I was somebody, or so I thought. Preachers all over the country knew me. God, look at all the good things I'd done.

My goodness, there was still so much confusion as to how and why such a thing like this happened. Where were Jacob's parents? I came from a house of order. More than once my daddy busted me on my lip. More than once, my mother collared me by my neck and sat me down in the chair when I misbehaved. I couldn't understand this experience with Jacob and his household. This experience appeared to be a horse of a different color, or so I thought. I began to recall memories from my childhood:

One day, after I was scolded by my father, I went down the stairs muttering and murmuring, "You're a no good rotten son of a bleep. If I didn't have to be here, I would not be. And after all, I didn't ask to be born and I don't know why I had to be born in such a family like this?" Oh, I could be disrespectful out in the cornfields because they couldn't hear me, but God knew what I was saying. My life was miserable. We lived in a house that was less than desirable, and I felt like I was just one of seven little children. I didn't matter. It seemed like I was the black sheep of the family; the one who was not liked by anybody anyway. They called me, "Big Mouth," " Blabber Mouth," and "Holier than Thou." They would make mean comments about my slight stature, such as, "Half the time you don't look like you're alive." Any chance I had, I told on them. I mocked them and I made fun of them. If I didn't like somebody, I stuck my tongue out, put my hands in my ears and waved my fingers at them with my tongue wiggling, saying, "Nah, nah, nah, nah."

When I was caught misbehaving or doing something I knew was wrong, I'd lie. Oh, I'd lie like a rug. "Wasn't me. I don't know how it happened?" I remember one time; I was downstairs messing with the water pump. The pump came on and I got scared. I put my hand up on the wheel, trying to stop it. Instead of stopping, it smashed my finger as it spun around and around. It crushed the bones in my finger and the blood was dripping everywhere. I ran up the stairs.

Mom saw my finger and asked, "How did this happen?"

"I don't know," I said, lying.

"Surely you know?" she said.

I stuck to my story, "I don't know. I went downstairs and something fell on my hand. It hurt it."

Even in the midst of pain, I was still lying. I broke the window and I'd look at her, "I don't know."

I told Momma I was doing well in school. I told her that I got "B's" on my tests. Every time momma asked, it was another "B." The day the report cards were handed out, here came the "F." Momma wanted to know, "How could that be? You've had a "B" all semester long and now you got a "F"?

Again, I used my favorite line, "I don't know?"

Is this why this happened, I wondered? Was I being punished for all the lies I told when I was a kid? Is this why I laying in this bed without a face? Is that why the rock had hit me? Was God punishing me because of those things? I thought I was a good man, but the more I reflected, the more I realized that I, too, did a lot of bad things as a kid. I was raised well, in a home with plenty of order and love, yet I was not a perfect child. I didn't do anything much worst than most kids, but just as bad as what others have done. Still, why was I the only one suffering in pain? Why didn't anybody else have a rock dropped on them. Why is God punishing me?

I thought about my behavior during adolescence, when I was older and able to drive. I used to go to prayer meetings when other kids were going to dances. Sometimes I told mom I was going to service, but I would actually go to see a girl. I was quite bold. I was a senior in high school but I was dating a freshman in college. I remember laying up in her bed, in her dorm room, and coming home and telling mom I'd been in a prayer meeting. I remember one night, I was sitting and drinking with one of my teachers before I had to drive down to Albany and pick mom up from work. She remarked, "Hmm, I spell berries."

"Yeah, we'd stopped and got some raspberries," I said, but the truth was I'd been drinking wine with one of the teachers. This was in high school.

Man, I thought I was a good person. Everybody thought I was good. I was always at church and always doing the right thing. I was always going to the right places, at the right times. But boy, when I could get away with something, I'd slip out the back and do whatever I thought I was big enough to do. Was I being punished because of the things I had done? Was this God's way of getting even with me? I just couldn't imagine it. I couldn't imagine that God was getting back at me for my previous behaviors.

I remember when I got my first checking account. I never seemed to be able to get the hang of balancing it. I wrote bad checks. I bounced checks and had to run around to get it cleaned up. I always wrote more checks than I had money in the bank to write, and I'd have to go and say,

I'm sorry, but…" "I'm sorry, but…" Sometimes, I'd just skip out of it and wouldn't even take care of the check. People would have to come after me to get their money and I had bills that I couldn't pay. It seemed like all my life I'd had bills that I couldn't pay. I always had bill collectors coming after me, threatening to sue me or take me to court. I'd have to scrounge up the money. I'd borrow $10 here, $100 there, and pay somebody a debt someplace else. Now I owed two people instead of one. Sometimes I couldn't pay them back. Was God punishing me for all those things?

"Heal me," I'd ask him many times. Every time I was in church and an altar call was given, I was always running to the altar and always saying, "Oh, God, forgive me because I know that I have sinned." I thought he had written that scripture, "For all have sinned and fallen short of the glory of God," especially for me. I knew I had sinned. Was God punishing me? I wasn't so good after all. Maybe I wasn't as good as I thought, or as good as people thought I was. So many times I let God down. Sometimes I let the people around me down. My first marriage didn't work out. I let my wife down. I also let my children down. I made a vow to God, "Till death do us part." Things got rough in our marriage and she said she wanted out. I told her, "Don't worry, you don't even have to leave," and I left. Was God punishing me for this?

Somehow, everything that I was doing seemed to be going wrong and I felt that maybe God was getting back at me. Maybe that was how he punished me. They said God was like a father. After all, when daddy got mad and he wanted to correct me, he'd turn my behind up, pulled my pants down and spanked the living daylights out of me, sometimes with the belt. Mommy got creative, she made us go out to get a willow branch, and then she told us to lie across the bed. She whipped me until my behind was red. It was a good thing Children's Services never saw it because, talk about welts, I had them down my legs, up my behind, and up my back.

I'll never forget the beating I got for smoking. I came home one day and Mommy asked, "You been smoking?"

"Not me," I said.

But the neighbors had already called up the street, "Shirley, your children are down here smoking, walking up the street, just smoking and puffing."

I got to the door and mommy said, "Were you smoking?"

"Oh, no, not me." I lied like a rug.

She said, "I don't believe you or your friends. You smell like smoke." Then she said that the neighbor had called and told her what they had seen. Boy, she beat me unmercifully. I danced around the bedroom. I tried to crawl under the bed, tried to get inside the closet. She beat me until I was purple, and then when daddy got home she told him what we had done, and he beat me some more. In no way did they abuse me as a child, but I got my share of beatings for lying and for doing stupid things. Was God punishing me for some of the things that I had done? Had he, in fact, really forgiven me? Could I be going through something so different or so removed from what other people have gone through? The rape victims, did they think like I am thinking? Did they wonder if they had gotten raped because of the things they had done? Then did they think that they were abandoned because of the things that they had done? As I laid in the bed, I felt like I was being tormented. Moment after moment, the torment continued.

Somewhere between life and death, every other hour, somebody came in my room, turning me, prodding me, poking me, forcing me to take pills, checking on this drip, checking on that drip, changing the dressing on this, and getting me ready to go back to surgery one more time. Then it was visiting time, and my room seemed to swell with people. Most were crying and sobbing. Everybody was telling me I was going to be okay, but they couldn't understand. I was the one laying in the bed. After they would leave, all I could think about was the issue of forgiveness.

I thought about the biggest, baddest, dirtiest, rottenest things that I had ever done. I mistreated a dear friend. Over the years, if I was ever in a financial jam, he would come to my rescue. He was a deacon in a small church in southern Ohio. God bless his soul. Every time I needed him, He was always there. Just a great friend. He was there to listen when the marriage was going bad. And whenever I couldn't pay my bills, he would send me money. Maybe God was punishing me for this? I borrowed money to take care of a bill and then I wouldn't pay him back. It really wasn't the first time I couldn't pay him back, but he just kept telling me it was okay. However, this time it was different. I wanted to pay him back, but I couldn't. So, in my shame, I stopped talking to him. I stopped accepting his phone calls, his help in my ministry, and any help that I needed in my family. In spite of this, he helped me pay my light bills, my gas bills, and he put food on the table for the kids while I was trying to finish up school. I had convinced myself that I was in this bed, not because of somebody else's deeds, but because of my own.

I wondered if anybody else has ever gone through this? Surely nobody else had ever had their face smashed by a rock going through the window of their car. What were the odds, a million to one maybe? What were the odds of this happening to anybody else quite like it happened to me? I'd never heard of this happening to anybody else. You couldn't convince me God wasn't punishing me. I was so good, so perfect, and so great. He was punishing me for that? I thought I made up for it when I asked him to forgive me and when I changed my attitude. I tried to be nice and I was nice. I even took care of my daddy when he got old. I don't know what happened. Why me? But it didn't happen to anybody else. It happened to me. In my mind, I couldn't understand why. I kept wondering if it was something I did or because of how badly I used to behave? I felt frantic inside, like I was searching, reviewing, examining every aspect of my life to find results to an unanswerable question. It continued to frustrate and anger me. It felt like insanity.

Even as a grown man, I do not understand. I don't know God, I just don't know. The children left home. They all moved away and they're not here with me anymore. Even the foster children are gone. I am alone. Why is this happening now? I don't know. I don't know why I'm sitting here in this bed in the hospital room. It's always dark because that is all that I can see. My tongue won't move. No sound comes out of my mouth. This is miserable. It's beyond my comprehension. I've preached a thousand times and read a thousand times: "…And forgive us our trespasses as we forgive those who trespassed…." Yet, I ask you

God, "Can I forgive somebody I don't even know? And why would you make me forgive him when I'm hurting so? When I'm blind and they took out one of my eyes and then they tell me they can't repair the other, why do you want me to have mercy upon him? My mouth doesn't work and neither does my nose. I'm sitting here in the dark. It hurts so badly, I have dreams of being in pain. My family is constantly praying. I don't even want to hear them pray any more. I feel so low. They told me to stop having a pity party, and that I ought to stop feeling sorry for myself. I want to respond that, if they thought I was having such a damned pity party, they ought to get in this bed and see how they'd like it. In fact what I wanted to say was, "Let me poke out your eyes, pluck off your nose, pull out your tongue, and see how much you would feel like praising God." The other day they wanted to sing a song, "I'm So Glad Trouble Don't Last Always." If I had a drum

I would have beat it to drown out the words. I felt like they didn't know what they were saying. I was glad trouble didn't last always, but it was bad enough trouble was lasting today. I had the pain to prove it.

I had to make it from morning to night. The good thing about being blind was that I didn't know whether it was morning or night. All I knew was that people kept changing all day long. "I'm your morning nurse. I'm your evening nurse." In between, all I knew was that God was punishing me. I couldn't go any lower. I thought to myself, "Maybe I'm dead and I'm not really living. And maybe I'm being put in hell and this is my torment, my fire." I felt like this was torment, but God just kept saying, "Forgive him. Forgive everybody."

It's a great thing that I couldn't get to the kid who threw the rock. Boy, I'd tell him a thing or two. I'd even take the rock and hit him in the head with it. I'd probably take their bikes and throw them over the bridge if I thought I could get away with it. Too bad I couldn't leave the hospital or find my way to the street. One positive thing about being here was the fact that I had stopped smoking. No one close to me even knew that I smoked cigarettes, I was so sneaky. I smoked at home. I smoked in my car. I smoked when nobody else was around. It didn't matter if I smelled like a tobacco factory. Every now and then I dropped an ash and it burned a hole in my pants. Oh, I thought people didn't see it, couldn't smell it and didn't know what I was doing. I'd just splash on a little more cologne.

Maybe God was punishing me for all the years he tried to get me to stop smoking and I just kept on doing it. Maybe he never forgave me for my transgressions, and this was his way of letting me know it? I just couldn't understand. It was far beyond what I could understand. Why on earth was I going through this? Was it ever going to end? Somehow, maybe the light would come on, maybe my tongue would get put back in, maybe my nose would get put back on, and I'd just be able to go home and function like everybody else. Maybe this is a dream from which I cannot wake? Most people left the hospital and they were always put back together, they were healed. I'm sure it was going to be that way for me.

I honestly don't know how long this torment went on. I don't know whether it was days, hours, weeks or months. I knew it just didn't end. I'd search myself. I prayed. I asked God to forgive me for everything that I had ever done and prayed that things could just get better. Even if I felt any better, nothing changed. I still couldn't see. I couldn't talk. I prayed that God would allow me to die.

Death would surely be easier than this torment.

I began to think about the sermons I had preached. I began to think about words that I had read. I heard God saying, "Johannes, you've got to learn, I want to glorify myself through you." I wondered, "Was he upset that I was mad at him?" I was mad at the doctors and the nurses. They hadn't been out there on that bridge. Someone could have prevented this from happening. Someone should have prevented this from happening. If so, I wouldn't have to be in this place. This place. I feel weakened from dealing with all this anger, all this pain.

"So look upon me, for my yoke is easy and my burden is light."

It wasn't light for me.

Do you hear me God? I just kept asking, "Do you hear me, God?"

He just kept saying, "Forgive."

I tried to remember all the times I asked God to forgive me. Would I forgive this kid? He wasn't asking me to forgive him or anything. Maybe he thought he wasn't worthy of my forgiveness either, or maybe he really didn't care at all. I hadn't even heard from him. I thought about the peace that I'd receive through death. It'd all be over.

All of the pain, agony, wondering, and the issue of forgiveness would be over. It seemed like it made sense to me. If I died, then I wouldn't have to deal with making peace with myself or with God, or any other little punk that would be so cruel to do what Jacob McNary did to me.

Again, God said, "Forgive."

Your will be done, Lord, I thought. Your will be done.

PHOTOS

Elaine, Johannes, Arthur, & George Jr.

One room Schoolhouse
Johannes, Elaine, George Jr. and Jean

The Christian Family

Brian & Dr. Christian at John Walsh Show

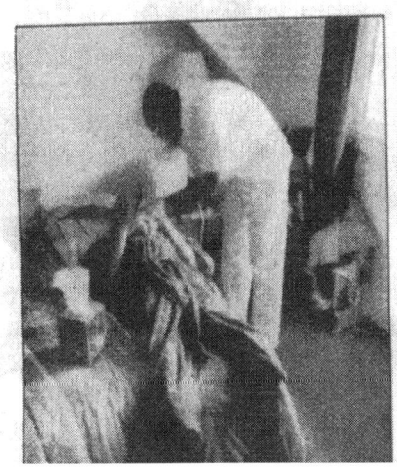

Nurse Abdul Sesay

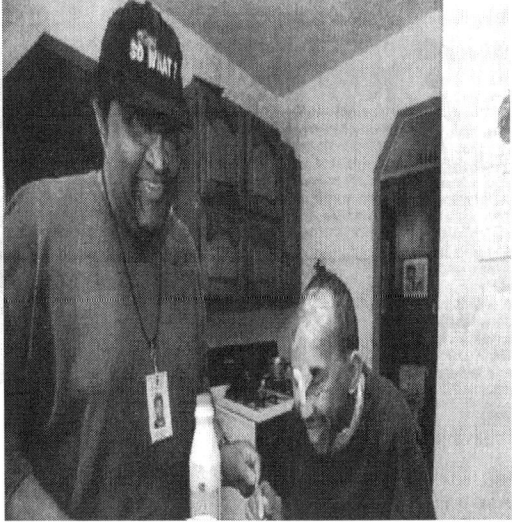

Personal aid, Mr. Willy Adams

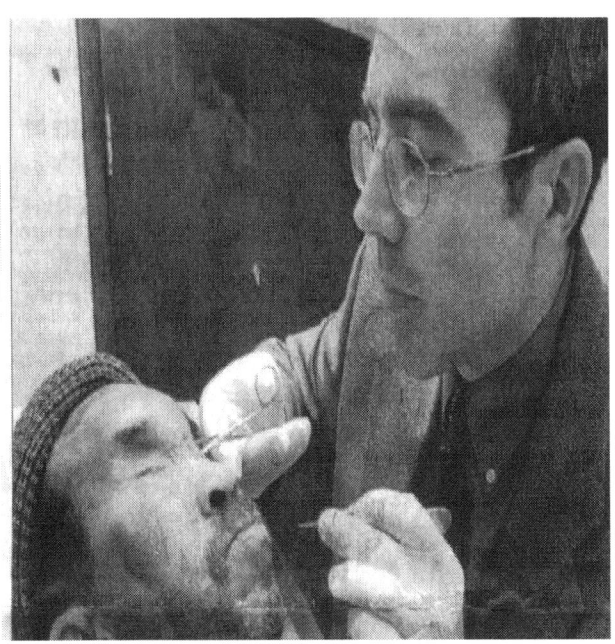

Plastic Surgeon, Dr. Schmidt

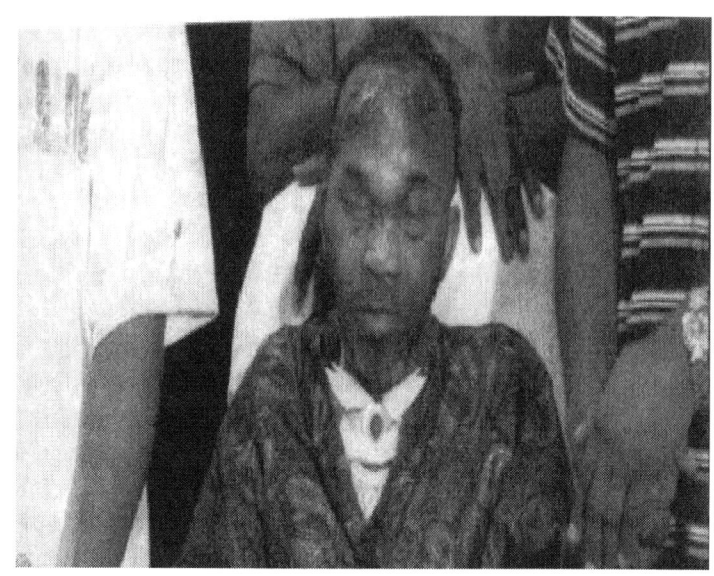

Early Days Of Recovery
Rev Dr Johannes J Christian

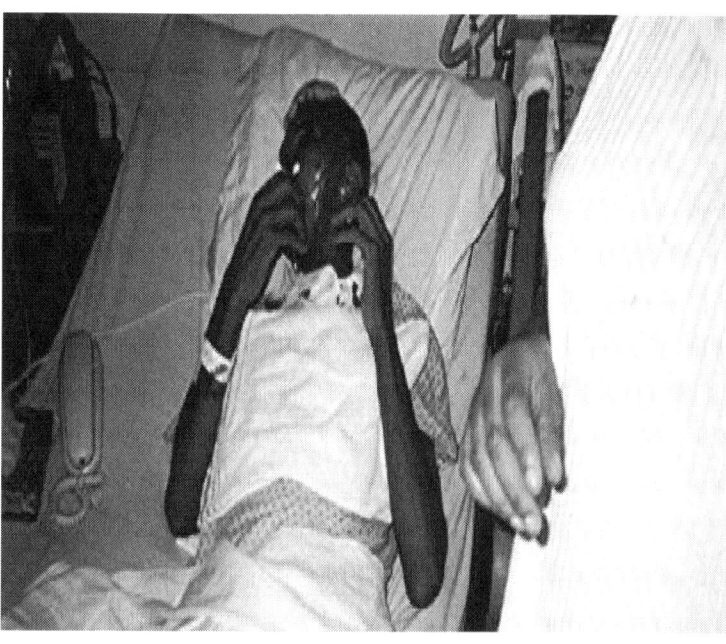

Rev Dr Johannes J Christian healing in hospital

(Copy of the second letter Rev. Christian wrote to Jacob McNary in prison.)

Reverend Dr. Johannes J. Christian
691 Lilley Avenue
Columbus, Ohio 43205

May 8, 2003

Dear Jacob,

I hope and pray that this letter finds you in good health and doing the will of our father. I continue to remember you in my prayers.

I hope that you remain strong in the Lord and in the power of His might. Are you still attending the Bible study group? Do you have the opportunity to work on your education?

I am continuing to make improvements in the adjustments in my life. Please continue to pray for me and my family.

I look forward to hearing from you as time allows.

Yours in Christ,

Johannes

> "The came Peter to him, and said, Lord, how oft shall my brother sin against me, and I forgive him? Till seven times? Jesus saith unto him, I say not unto thee, until seven times, but until seventy times seven."
>
> - Matthew 18-22

"I Will Survive"

My feelings were probably no different than anybody else's, given my circumstances. My emotions ran a gamut from anger, anxiety, lethargy and depression.

From what I have been told by my family, almost from Day One after the accident, when I regained consciousness, I seemed to be in control of my thought processes. I was able to say that I knew that I was in the hospital. I was told that I was in an accident and I understood that. I remembered that Brian was also in the car with me and I had a great concern for him. Throughout the day, I moved in and out of a sleep pattern, probably because of the medication and severe trauma and pain that I was experiencing. I felt the need to touch, to hold onto that which I knew was constant in my life, for example, my son, Tyrone, and my sister, Martha. I remember feeling frustrated because I could not move around, but I could sense that there was lot of movement about me. I could not be a part of what was going on. I was keenly aware of the persistent darkness that consumed me like a thick fog from which there was no escape.

I am told that when I was able to, I tried to be in control of my life. I am told that from the outside looking in, it seemed as though I never lost that desire to participate in the things that affected me. Even from the early stages, several days after the accident into my recovery, I wanted to know exactly what was the diagnosis or prognosis? I wanted to hear for myself the severity of the damage to my face, my body. I wanted to know that the doctors communicated with me, and that they were telling me the same things that they were telling my family members. I knew at that time that decisions needed to be made concerning my life and that those decisions were ultimately decisions that would be made by my children. I remember being confident in the ability of my children to do what was right, but I was overcome with a deep feeling of dread concerning what the future held for me. Would I walk again without assistance? Would I be able to jog again? What about hang-gliding, which I picked up as a hobby just a few months prior to my accident? Oh, God, I'll never be able to see our property on the Virgin Islands, which has been in our family for decades, and which was a place of solitude and peace for me.

There was a strong feeling that I wouldn't survive at times. This fact hit me when I requested that my attorney come to the hospital to arrange for my son, Tyrone, to assume Power of Attorney over my affairs. There must have been some recognition of how much I have done for my children by their responses toward me. Almost in a joking manner, I told my sons, George and Tyrone, that they needed to get good jobs and go to work to care for themselves and their families, because I would no longer be able to provide for them. It was funny, because in essence, I really was not taking care of either one of them at that juncture. Both of them were self-sufficient and living on their own. I am not sure where that idea came from? Maybe it felt like I was always giving them something.

There was always so much excitement and activity going on around me, but it was still difficult to stay connected with what seemed to be the "Outside" world, as my blindness and the trauma I experienced drew me inward. It was also hard for me to keep track of days and times. It seemed as though I knew that it was Sunday or Saturday. Maybe it was

Saturday or Sunday. Special attention was being given to my room, and me, and it seemed as though there were people who continued to move about. I didn't have a sense of whether it was nighttime or morning. However, I continued to ask the nurses, as they came in and out, what time it was when they gave me my medication. But the feeling that I was experiencing was that they were preparing the room for visitors. Then there were streams of people, voices that sounded familiar. Of course I could not see any faces, but I could always tell whether it was somebody who knew me real well or somebody who was a professional by the way they addressed me. I had a fear that I was losing touch with who I was.

Because of my condition, my blindness, and my inability to interact with others in a more conventional manner, I often felt like I was being put on display. I almost felt like I was a commodity in a Kroger's grocery store. In the way that people select their produce in the store, there was a sense of people coming into my hospital room and poking and prodding and picking at me. I do not know how to express that in words other than saying I felt like maybe I was the "Special of the Week." Besides constantly picking at me, people also moved me about quite a bit, and the loss of control this brought was quite unnerving. I had no power of my life; it's like I didn't really control where I was going, what I was thinking, or what I was doing. I didn't even have a say in what I was eating. My condition wouldn't permit me to do it, so I ate Jell-O and drank pineapple juice. Lord, am I a child again?

As I lay in the bed, though my mind was racing about, I was able to think about a lot of issues in my own life. I felt really frustrated because I did not have a sense of time or space. Everything was just utter darkness. I asked myself, "Was I going to be in the dark for the rest of my life? Just blackness?" I remember asking questions of people, "Am I ever going to see light again or is everything always going to be dark? Black?" The loss of my vision left me with a great big void. I felt like I was on display. I heard the comforting words from my family and friends as they came into the room. I almost felt like I could feel their shock at my condition. I must have looked a mess. I continued to ask, "What do I look like?" People would respond, "Oh, you do not look very bad. You are okay. You are pretty banged up, but not bad." I knew they weren't telling me the whole truth. At one point I remember trying to touch my face, and I felt like Humpty-Dumpty, except it would take more than the king's men to put me back together.

People came and they would only stay for a short while and then they'd go. It always made me wonder. I was really concerned about what I looked like but no one was really telling me what I look like. I just rested.

My family's presence was a blessing to me emotionally. I had a real need to touch and to hold on to them. When my children came in, I just had to hold on to them. When I say hold on, I mean grabbing their hands, holding, and clutching their hands. They clutched mine in return, but I couldn't communicate too much with them. I was not able to talk. I was not able to write. I am told that for the first two days we were using a tapping system. When someone asked me a question, I tapped my response with my fingers. If I was in pain, I could squeeze their hand. If things were kind of okay, I could maybe stroke part of their hand with my index finger. I wanted to move about. I was not use to lying still. Being somewhat high-strung since my youth, I never sat in the same place for two minutes.

Somewhere in the first week, I kept thinking that I could just lift the bandages off of my eyes and I would be able to see again. One night, I guess I went totally berserk. I tried to pull all of the tubes out of my chest. They said I was quite a mess. I had the staff running around the hospital. I was feeling quite moody. Although I knew that people were praying for me, I also had to pray myself. I really felt a need to pray. God, why are you doing this to me? What's your purpose?

During this time in the hospital, my mind was very mixed up and all over the place. Although the hospital took very good care of me throughout my stay, my perceptions were altered and somewhat blurred. The hospital felt like a very foreign place. It felt like a very unstable and disorganized place to be. It did not seem like a professional establishment from my skewed vantage point. It seemed very loosely run. I do not know why I felt that way. In my mind, the hospital was like a zoo. I do not know where that feeling came from, but it was in my brain and that was what I felt. I cannot put a picture with it. I did not think of it as an agency run by medical professionals. I felt like everyone was too laid back, but maybe the pain medicine was altering my perceptions. I always had a lot of questions and concerns that seemed to go unanswered by the staff. For example, I did not think that they were sure where they were going medically. What were they doing? I had a lot of questions.

I felt like I was in a little wagon being pulled around. My bed was parked here for a minute, and then I was moved over there. I felt like I was in a garden. I knew I couldn't be, because I was in a hospital. I am in a hospital. I knew I was sick and yet I was not sick because of something so typical like an upset stomach. I was sick because I was hit in the head. I heard that over and over. Sometimes people were squeezing my hands or they were rubbing my shoulder. I did not feel anybody touching me from my neck up. It seemed like things got calmer when people were around me, especially when my family was around me. The first couple of days, it seemed as though everybody was always there. They were coming in and out. In the midst of all my foreign experiences, my mother was a constant source of strength during my recovery. My mom came in the room. It must have been late at night. It must have been in the evening. Mom was there and I could always feel her presence. My mom is here. She is did not show any kind of fear, although much later she told me the sight of me frightened her very much. She just stroked me. It was like she took over. It was almost like when I was a child. You know, Mom came in and no matter what was wrong, everything was all right because Mommy made it all right. Even though her voice was not strong, I could hear her voice or just background noises. I knew people were working all around me; and I was aware of beeping noises. Still, she did not have a sense of fear.

It meant a lot to me when my daughter, Vanessa, visited me. I could tell when Vanessa came to see me, because she was always rubbing my arm. I could feel her touching me. It was like I could feel people on both sides of me. I felt like I was on this wagon, real low to the ground, and people were looking down at me. I couldn't see anything, but I kept asking, "Am I going to see again?" Sometimes it seemed like they were giving me information and other times it seemed like they were not. I would ask, "How severe is the damage," and, "Where is Brian?" I sensed the presence of people outside of my family in my room. The second day after the accident, I remember hearing the voices of my friends, Angie Cornelius and Brother Hugh Black. They were members of Mt. Olivet Baptist Church. It was not Sunday, so maybe it was Tuesday or Wednesday. Angie always called me Rev. Christian. I could hear her voice clearly, "You are going to be all right."

It was just a constant stream of people. People from my job, from my former job, from the State, all came to visit. I remember little mental snapshot. Everybody that came seemed to want to touch me. If they were not rubbing my hands, they were rubbing my feet. There were people praying. My mind was all over the place. I had many questions. I wondered, "Is my car okay?" The day seemed like it would never end. I guess it never ended because I did not know when it began. One minute my mind seemed clear. The next minute my mind seemed cloudy and I was groggy. I wanted to go home. I have been told that they had been running me back and forth to surgery. Every day there was a surgery. A couple times a day there was a surgery, but I had no sense of what they were doing. I did not feel any different. I did not feel them working on my head but I knew that they were doing something. That was what they were telling me. I had a sense that I was going to be all right. Maybe I felt that way because everybody kept telling me I was going to be all right.

I couldn't say I knew when Day One ended and where Day Two or Day Three began. The first day of consciousness had to be Monday, the day that I arrived at the hospital. I was back to that feeling of being rolled around in my little wagon. I was being pulled around, being parked here, then moved over there. They pushed the bed and the bed was just rolling. It rolled around. I do not know how much of my experience was imagined. I felt like I was able to smell. I could smell flowers. I felt like the little guy in the commercial for Wal-Mart. It is the little dot that rolls around the store. He is just a head with a smiley face, a great big smiley face. I was not smiling though. I guess I just had a vision of that little dot moving around. I felt Vanessa, and my other daughters, Reecy and Samara. All my daughters are with me now. This has got to be Day Three or Four that I have been in the hospital. "We are here, Daddy. We are here," they would say. "Do you know who this is? If you know who this is, squeeze my hand," my daughter said. I was squeezing. It was Reecy, my baby daughter. I could feel them squeezing my hands. I heard voices saying, "You are going to be okay,

Daddy." I was squeezing them back thinking to myself, "All right, I am squeezing you back."

I wanted to be okay. It must have been Day Three. I was feeling somewhat stronger. I needed a pencil. I wanted to write. I was never very good at spelling. Boy, what a challenge this was. I had to write on this paper. I do not think they understood what I was thinking. Now all my children were in the room. They were asking me questions about what I wanted done with things. I wanted to make sure that the church was running. I wanted to make sure that the house was running. Who was watching my house? Who was watching my puppy, Hezekiah, who I just acquired a couple months before the accident? "Is Hezie okay?" I remember thinking, writing. I must have been getting stronger.

It was near the end of the week. I knew that I was not in Columbus. I was in Dayton. I never made it back to our city. It would have been easier if they took me back to the Ohio State University Hospitals. That was a big hospital. It must have been better than this little dinky place they had me in. They did not seem very professional around here and they just came and went, as they wanted. I still felt quite mixed up. All my thoughts were jumbled together. Now my brother, Arthur, and his wife, Betsy, were there. It had to be the first day.

God, I couldn't get past the first and second day of feeling so strong. I felt like Art had laid on top of me. He was always my little brother. No matter what we went through, we always went through it together. I began to remember my childhood. I thought about the past and all the things that Art and I used to do together. I was lying there in the bed. I guess I should've been concentrating on getting better, but I was lost in memories of the past. I remember riding in that old Pontiac with Art, traveling back and forth to work at the Holiday Inn and eating ice cream. "How am I remembering all this?" I asked myself. I almost couldn't tell what was a dream and what was reality.

I felt like I was being used for medical experiments. I was like a guinea pig. With the frequent opening and closing of my bedroom door, I felt like I was being locked up. Here came the doctors and nurses. They were locking me away and then they'd come and get me. They'd bring me out, and then they'd put me back. It almost felt like I was on top of the roof. I got some sunshine. This was a weird, weird feeling. It seemed like they had given me all these options. I could do this, that or other. It seemed like I was making the decisions, yet I did not know what I was deciding. Nothing really made sense. I did not know if they knew what they were doing. I felt like I was not in control. I felt like I was in prison. That is what it was like. I knew there were nurses and I could tell the differences between how they treated me. Sometimes people seemed very friendly, almost romantic, touching and feeling and probing and prodding, and then here came the mean crew. It was almost like they had chains and whips. Sometimes it felt like people were hurting me. I felt like Kunta Kinte from Alex Haley's "Roots." These were the weirdest thoughts that I could ever imagine. Although I could guess, I had no idea what day it was or how long I have been here. All I keep asking was, "What day is it," and, "How long have I been in here?" It was a deep blur. I was moving way ahead of myself.

This had to be Day Seven because it was Saturday or Sunday. Lord, there were so many people visiting me. They were here for a minute and then they were gone. Bob Barboski from my job came to visit. His voice did not sound very strong. Everybody was whispering. I did not feel like I was dead, but I did not feel like I was alive. Stacy McErris, my secretary from Civilian Conservation Corps, also came to see me. I could feel her presence, but she did not stay for long. She was here and gone. Elder Helen Jean Stewart and her nephew, Reverend David, also came. It must have been God's House of Prayer because they were praying. They were praying in tongues and I am felt a sense of strength coming from them. Maybe that was what I was doing. I was drawing strength from the people that were standing around me. It was like I could feel their moods. It was an interesting thought. When people came in, I became more conscious of my surroundings. When people were not around, I did not feel anything. I had a sense of needing to talk to God. I was trying to decipher some of the feelings that I had. I had never felt so mixed up in all my life and even when trying to remember what I felt, it is still mixed up. I know I kept making decisions and every time my children asked my opinion, "Yep, that sounds like a good idea," I would reply.

There is one voice, the voice of the doctor that seemed so calm. It was a calming and soothing voice. He talked soft and very calm. In a sense, it was not that they were moving me. It was that they went away and then they came back. That doctor again, had the same voice. I am on display.

I felt the need to pray. I just felt the need to talk to God. If I could just get through this, I would be okay. I am not sure where that was coming from. Was this need coming from the people visiting or was it coming from within me? I felt like I needed to be strong. I did not think that I could tell people that I was afraid, but I was. There were a lot of things that I needed people to do. I couldn't do them for myself.

I thought about Brian and J.R., my foster sons. I wondered, "Who is taking care of them? Where are they?" They are good children. I wondered how they were doing at home. "Who is watching my house?" "Where is George?" "Is George staying at my house?" I wanted someone to find Georgie. I could tell that my children were in the hospital room. I needed their support, because they had just rolled me in for surgery. As the anesthesiologist entered the room, I felt the need to pray. I thought about my family, "Please pray. Pray for me." I wanted everybody to pray for me. I felt cold hands against my skin. I followed directions and repeated, "100, 99, 98…" My body was temporarily at peace from the questions and confusion. All was silent.

I remember waking up from surgery, and my awareness increased each time. Each time, I remember thinking, "I'm still alive." Ultimately, I would undergo more than 30 surgeries to repair and rebuild my face. Each time, I remember thinking, "I will survive."

(Copy of the third letter Rev. Christian wrote to Jacob McNary in prison.)

Reverend Dr. Johannes J. Christian
691 Lilley Avenue
Columbus, Ohio 43205

October 24, 2003

Dear Jacob,

I hope that this letter finds you in the best of health. How are your parents doing? You have not mentioned them in your letters. I pray that things are going well with them.

I hope that you don't mind me writing you? I think that it is good therapy for the two of us. It is my heart's desire that you will learn to love yourself unconditionally, I think that this will be easier for you if you know that I am not only forgiving you for your actions, but I pray that God will continue to help me to love you as I love myself.

I am convinced that God's grace of forgiveness given to us is an example of the measure of forgiveness that He requires of us. Jesus said, "My peace I leave with you," and I trust you are able to find the peace of God in your life. I find a great deal of comfort in the word of God. Is it comforting to you? Are you still going to Bible study? What are you studying?

We had special services at our church every night last week. We remembered you in prayer that God will strengthen you and use you as a vessel in his service.

Sincerely with Love,

Johannes J. Christian

> "But there is forgiveness with thee,
> that thou mayest be feared."
>
> *- Psalms 130:4*

Ripples of Life

The fallout of my accident not only impacted my life forever, it also changed the lives of those closest to me, including my family, friends and members of my congregation. My accident also spawned ripples that changed the way I relate to my community and it with me.

One of the things that I have continued to hear from my children is the total devastation of how this can happen to their dad. I was not a perfect dad in any way shape or form, and in my eyes I feel that there are many things that I could have done differently. I might have been more gentle with my children, more loving, or even more honest in some areas of my own personal life. But, nevertheless, in the eyes of my children, I was a man that seemed bigger than life to them. At first glance I did not understand such a statement because to to see me, I am all of 5-feet-5 and during my children's lives never weighed more than 125 pounds. By the time I had reached aged 50, even before the accident, I had probably begun to look somewhat emaciated because of other medical concerns. Yet, to hear my children talk you'd think I was bigger than life. During conversations with all my children, particularly my daughters, Vanessa,

Clarice and Samara, they have expressed to me that, to them, I seemed to be the man with all of the answers. And that no matter what it was they were encountering in life, they could rest assured that, if they asked, they would get an answer from me that made sense and was of value. If it were a question that involved a life decision, such as identifying a chief mentor or a particular job, or whether it was a question about how to prepare a meal or repair something, I would have an answer for them. I must say that this kind of scenario occurred repeatedly over the course of our lives together prior to the accident. This book is not about their individual lives, but I do want to discuss the emotional impact my accident and battle for survival has had on all of our lives. For my daughters, I think it has been an opportunity for them to go through a spiritual transformation of seeking a religious kind of experience or relationship with our Lord, Jesus Christ. It's not that they did not know religion. Believe me, being the children of a preacher, they did their fair share and time in churches. From the moment we opened our raggedy, storefront church in Columbus, Ohio, they all hauled Bibles and hymnals and all the instruments back and forth every Sunday, and then set up church waiting for people to come. Then they would stand at the door as ushers, then run to the front of the church to sing in the choir. They would be there for prayer, and then be there to assist their father after he wore himself down from preaching. In some cases it meant they not only have to drive me to the church, and drive me home and then wait for me to kind of revive myself after I had come back to life from total exhaustion. Even though they had this in-church experience, I do not know that they actually had a relationship with Christ as much as a relationship with their own dad.

Since the accident, my children have developed a rather pointed relationship with Christ. How, you ask? Well, from the earliest time of my recollection following the accident, and whenever any of them would come into the room (including my beloved daughter-in-law, Yolanda, and son-in-law, Arthur) I was always cognizant of the fact that they were not only there to give me physical and emotional support, but I could feel their prayerful support as well. I remember their verbal expressions of faith, points they had heard me express throughout their lives about how to plead the blood of Jesus to be rid of Satan and whatever controls he was trying to dictate in our lives. Even though I could not see them, I could feel their spirits, and I could sense their tears as they tried to make sense of everything as they prayed. Today, I am so grateful that, at a time when they should have been in utter despair and utter desperation, they were like children who had leaned on one another and called on a power that was greater than them. I truly believe it was through their crying out that they were able to say to God, "We trust you. We trust that you will help us get through this situation and we will be stronger in faith because of it."

I know this because as I grew stronger, I asked them, "Was there ever a time when you felt like I was not going to pull through? Was there ever a time when you thought that I was not going to make it?" On a conscious level, I do not believe any of them were ever to the point where they thought that I would not make it. Whether it was that their mind just could not comprehend my passing, or whether they actually felt that God would not let them down, but they believed if they prayed for me to live, I would live.

It was during the critical hours immediately after my accident that my sons, Tyrone and George, my sisters, Jean and Elaine, and my foster son, Brian, were present. What they saw had to be quite unnerving. I learned much later that Tyrone called his wife, Yolanda, who stayed home with their children, to tell her that he could not recognize his own father on an emergency room table. He described the bloody sight he saw, how there was no skin left on my face from the top of my forehead down to my lips, which had fallen off. How there was only a hole where my nose and eyes had been, how the rock eradicated everything. "Daddy doesn't have a face," my son told his wife. "He doesn't appear to be living and I don't know how he is going to live. There's nothing left of him. He's just gone." Yolanda tried to comprehend what she was hearing, saying, "What do you mean? How can he not have a face?" Tyrone replied again, "He doesn't have a face. It's all gone. There's just nothing there but just a kind of masses of broken up tissue."

I do not know how you express what a child is feeling when they are watching a loved one who has literally been blown apart. I would imagine that it was kind of like seeing a loved one that maybe came home from the battlefield having been hit by a piece of shrapnel or a bomb exploding and blowing off part of an individual. I really recollect that perhaps what my children were seeing in me would resemble that of a person coming home from war, and consequently, I would think that their feelings would be much the same as those that most family members would have when a person came home.

On one hand, you can understand the victim of war, who felt the consequences of military engagement. But for their father who was just driving home from a family gathering, who had just been together with the entire family, this was not a normal reaction. I was not coming home from war. I had always been a man of peace and not a man of war, and they had never seem me so much as in a fight or an argument with another individual, so this would not have been something that would have been expected. But I think because it comes as a rather unexpected event that it is one for which there is no prior preparation, and when one tries to come to grips with it, it leaves a real void for an answer. While I think that on one hand that they really never thought that I would die, I think that in those crucial moments of the night that they really did not expect that I would live.

I know that as my daughter, Vanessa, and her husband, John, drove from Peoria, Ill. with their children, Johannes II, Marie and little John – the baby whose dedication was my reason for being in Peoria – there were feelings of guilt. They tried to reason that had I not come to Peoria in the first place that this would not have happened. Since my recovery, I've tried to tell them that, no matter where I was or what I was doing there should be no feelings of guilt because the circumstances under which this horrific crime occurred had nothing to do with our family. It did, however, have everything to do with the powers that be, and the battle that waged in the mind of Jacob McNary. Nevertheless, I know Vanessa struggled with that feeling that somehow she was partially responsible for the accident. It tested her faith, which was and still is strong. As a young adult, Vanessa had given her life to the Lord and had similar urgings to be all that God wanted her to be. She had come to grips with being a woman of God, being a spokesperson for God, a preacher for God if you will, and so she has allowed this horrific experience to deepen her faith and deepen her walk with the Lord. You know, she is a lot like me in many ways. She has a real desire to be spiritually motivated and to have that Pentecostal experience and baptism of the Holy Ghost, and the ability to speak in tongues and also the ability to have the power of God move through her through the laying on of hands. She has become very much a woman of prayer and even if she would be standing around me in the room and while she was out of the room, she would be on the phone talking with the other saints from her church, asking them to pray and to continue to be in prayer and allowed them to encourage her to be the woman of faith that God wanted her to be. I was so aware of her standing around my bed and touching my shoulder, because nobody could touch my head. She and others rubbed my arms, which had

the least amount of scars. Vanessa would stand and touch me, praying, struggling to tell me that I needed to pull through, that I could pull through, that would pull through, while at the same time trying express to her young children, Johannes, 4, and Marie, 2, that Grandpa had an accident and got a very bad boo-boo.

For my son, George, the accident left him with more questions than answers. At the time, he was enrolled at the Circleville Bible College in Circleville, Ohio, which is located about 26 miles south of Columbus. He was pursuing religious education and playing basketball. He would ultimately leave his studies to help care for me after I got home from the hospital. I know in our conversations during my recuperation, he really wanted to know why God would allow this to happen, especially if God is suppose to be all-knowing and all-kind. I think to George it was the how's and the whys that tormented him the most. How could He allow this to happen? There were times in George's life when he and I went around and around about erratic behaviors I believed were out of line for a young man. And now, somebody else's child did such an unthinkable act that it was difficult for George to comprehend. I do not believe that he lost his faith. I think it was more a crying out to God, more of the fear and anger of my condition. But, he continued to cry out. It was very, very difficult for him to come back and forth to the hospital. Often, Vanessa and Tyrone had to go find George to bring him to the hospital, to pull himself together enough to come up and at least be present. He was reluctant not because he did not love me, not because he did not want to be there, but because emotionally it was just so difficult for him to see me lying there helpless, nearly lifeless. It spawned such profuse anger in him that he did not know how to react.

Of all my children, I knew George really wanted to track Jacob down and cause him as much bodily injury as he caused me. George could have done it, too, as God blessed George with much physical size and strength. George could have, would have ground Jacob McNary to a pulp, if he could have gotten close enough to him. Confusing these emotions were the plethora of notes I kept giving him pleading for calm, pleading for forgiveness, pleading that he turn the other cheek. On one hand, I think George wanted to hear that. On the other hand, I think he wanted to say, "Daddy, could we just be real and that maybe if we could just be real and you would allow me to just take this kid outside and knock him around a little bit, if you would not feel better, at least I would."

    I thank God for the people George had around him at the Circleville Bible College. I know his friends and his teachers were very much in prayer for me and they were very much in prayer with George. I know they encouraged him and tried to help him get through this situation. I know that both of his buddies, Jay and Sam, tried to support him to the best of their ability and understanding. Sam, Jay and George had been lifelong friends. They had gone through high school together, and Sam and George were in the same college and going through their basketball careers together. Jay had taken another track, but was still very much a part of their lives. These two young men had lived in and out of our house, and George had lived in and out of their houses. They were inseparable, so I know my accident was as Earth shaking to them as it was for George. George never expressed his emotions in an outward manner, he always seemed to carry things inside. Even as a child, he was not a talker, and when he talked, he did not talk in long, flowing sentences. He would just get to the point, say what it was he had to say and spend the rest of the time in silence. I think he had a difficult time expressing what was going on in his mind following the accident. Even so, I will never forget lying in the hospital bed, and George standing at the foot of the bed rubbing my toes telling me that everything would be all right. He never went into any biblical soliloquies or any long dissertations, speeches or any rambling, babbling kind of words. He would just say, "Daddy is going to be all right." And I think there was more power in his touch than even in his words. I do not even remember whether he had his great big bushy Afro or his long braids. I would say I am blind and I could not see it then, but there were just two extremes that he would have either a big bushy 'fro or his long braid. But one thing I do know is that his love and his heart were there whether he could pull himself to come to the room or not, his thoughts and his prayers were there and I know that from him I gleaned an awful lot of strength because of the love that he had for me. And even though other people may not always understand him, no matter what he said or did, I could always try to figure out where my George was.

My two truck-driving daughters, Samara and Clarice, had the longest drive. They had to come all the way from Denver to Dayton, and talking about their experience would be quite difficult. You see Clarice was always my emotional young lady. She was my crier. She was my deep-thought lady, my one that always really wanted the most to please. She always got great satisfaction knowing that I was pleased with the decisions she made. It really was difficult to see her as she attempted to be this grown-up woman at 20, watching her father lay in the bed having gone through such an experience. Clarice and Vanessa were emotional supports for each other throughout the ordeal. On the other hand, Samara, my eldest child, is very much a take-charge kind of spirit, and all of my children look to her for guidance and leadership. That no doubt had to be a great challenge as all my children were at a lost as to what to do next. She had to be both mother and big sister at once, and she refused to allow anyone to see her waiver a bit. She could not allow them to see her crying and falling apart, but had to be there to help them make the decisions that needed to be made. I do not know where she was emotionally or spiritually. I believe her emotions got lost in her concern for everybody else around her; while she has always been somewhat bossy, she stepped up in pulling everybody in line and help them understand what would be expected of them as this whole thing unfurled. I think they all tried not to get too far down the road as to whether or not I was going to die or stay alive. I think everybody was trying to take it one moment at a time, in the hope that if they got through that moment, they could get through the next moment and so on.

I understand the thought process of sustenance that permeated everyone's minds that were present at the hospital with me. There was the feeling that, by the time we reached the next morning, having made it through the night; we can make it through the next day. Looking at this chunks of time created a sense of relief that perhaps this particular storm was going to come to some kind of end, and perhaps this emotional roller coaster was sooner or later going to come to a halt and we would all be able to get off. I know that for the first few days there was very little relief for my family. For me, however, there seemed to be a prevailing calmness as I lay there in a semi-vegetative state. I did not have to breath on my own because I had a ventilator helping me to breath. Since I did not have a mouth that was working properly, I did not get to talk very much. Needless to say, I didn't have to focus my sights on anything in particular. I could not tell whether it was morning or night. All I did was just lie there with a feeding tube in my stomach so I probably was the least emotional person in the room. I was so doped up for the pain that I do not remember very much of anything, and yet I remember so much of the comfort and strength that I received from each of my five children as they walked in and out of the room. Yes, I have said five children. I never want to exclude my daughter-in-law, Yolanda, who continued to run back and forth, and served as a pillar of strength for my son, Tyrone. Every time they would walk in and out of the room, I think it enabled me to muster up the strength to live and not die.

These were the children that I had held in my arms since birth and most of them have been there through all of the trying times in our lives, and there had been many trying times. While each of them probably believe they were the worst of all of my children, I would say that all of them had their moments of being good and all of them had their moments of being bad, but none of them were probably as bad as they think they were. Truly, it did not matter what they had gone through with their father, I knew that they were all there for me.

My accident also had ripple affects with my brothers and sisters, especially the ones who stood vigil with my children at the hospital. We had grown up together in one house. We had gone through the experience of being poor and struggling through school and raising our families, and we have a bond between us that is very strong. Don't get me wrong, we do not always agree, but the love we feel for one another is rock solid. Having stated this, I know it was very difficult for my brothers and sisters to realize that whatever happened to me, it was my children who must take charge of the situation. I'm sure they fought the urge to take control, and forced themselves to take a step back to encourage and nurture my children to make the right decisions with the information they received from my doctors. But they did it, and just as I received such strength from the presence of my children in the room, so it was with my sisters and my brothers. Each nourished me with love and strengthened my will to survive. Each provided nuggets of the great faith we had been given from our praying mother; nuggets that we received from watching Daddy go through the many medical challenges in his life, including stomach ailments and a severe heart condition. I know for a fact that the prayers of my sisters, Jean and Elaine, provided me with added strength because they refused to let me go. They would not dream of saying that I was not going to make it, and would not allow anybody else to say to I was not going to make it. Although I know Elaine was bouncing on the phone sharing with other relatives what was going on, both her heart and her concern was there that her brother was going to make it. Jean, on the other hand, focused on helping my children understand that she was there for them, and that they could make the decisions they needed to make. How difficult it had to be for her to stand around my bed. Not only did Jean have to bear watching me suffer, she had to be there for my mother. You see Jean was already caring for my mother, who had previously suffered a stroke as we buried my father. Now she was doing triple duty. She was trying to work, trying to take care of Mom, and running back and forth between Columbus and Dayton to make sure I got what I needed. But she did it.

There was my eldest brother, Godfrey, with whom I had gotten closer following his heart attack and subsequent recovery. In fact, he always told me I helped save his life because I got him to the hospital on time for the doctors to help him. By the time I was in high school, Godfrey (who's nickname is Mickey or Mick) had already been out of the house and in the Army, so while we had some childhood experiences, we were never close at home even though I visited with him as a young adult in Philadelphia when I was in college. However, since I was trying to suck up religion as well as party in the City of Brotherly Love, we never really got to know each other and never were very close. Still, following my accident I received strength from him. Mick, who always had a wonderful singing voice, came to me in the hospital just a few hours after my arrival. Not a talkative man, Mick is very emotional and I gained strength from his presence.

My youngest brother, Arthur, and his wife, Betsy, live in Urbana, Ohio, a small town near Dayton, and were constantly with me. Two years separate us, and we were close as children and as adults. With a year separating Elaine, Art and I, I'm not sure we ever really grew up. We still tend to treat each other like we are still children. I know Art spent a lot of time crying and a lot of time biting his lip and praying for me after the accident. Very religious, Art has a solid relationship with Christ and this helped him gather strength to share with me. I also know he had the other members of his church in Springfield praying for me. Every time Art came into my room, I tapped into his faith. He would sit and hold me and his presence comforted me. I really believe he would have traded place with me if he could have. Sometimes a feeling of helplessness was so great for him that he did not know quite what to do with it. He'd always say, "This is your little brother, Art" as if that was just going to make everything all right. Little did he know that every time he said it, it just gave me a vote of confidence that we were going to make it because that is all we ever said to each other as kids. I have to admit that when he came into my hospital room, I received flashbacks of some of our adventures together, such as pulling dirty dishes through the dishwasher at the Holiday Inn where we worked together, getting soaked and having to get out of our wet clothes and drive home in a car with no heat. I thought about the time we spent at a football game or hanging out with Bob Fota, our English teacher, or the moments we shared driving back and forth to Albany to pick up Mom after she got off work at Midnight, and still getting up at 5 a.m. for school. I even remembered our trips from Upstate New York to Montreal, when we'd drive his beat up Pontiac to meet buddies we worked with at the Gideon Putman, a big fancy hotel where we were waiters. I do not know why at a time when my life was really falling apart that his being present gave me such hope to live?

I know someone is reading this expecting that I am going to be very spiritual at this point, but I am just trying to be very real. I laid in the bed seeing nothing but darkness and not knowing what was going on with me. Whenever people came into the room, I would zap strength from them and fond memories. And that was real. My nieces and nephews would come one by one; and I'd thank God for our big family. I have to stop and say that I wondered that, if we had a smaller family would I have had less of a desire to live. I definitely would have had less people from which to zap strength. My niece, Christine, who I had watched and almost had become a surrogate father after the death of my sister, Patty, was there. To her I was more than an uncle. I was someone who was a father figure and a grandfather to her children. I had also been there to provide financial relief from time to time, when she needed help paying her rent or to fix her car. It was like she was trying to tell me that she intended to pay me back, and I had better survive so she could do so. In her presence, I could sense her saying through her sobs, "You were there for me when I got married. You made my flowers. You were there for me when I did not know how to make decisions. You were there and you have got to make it." She gave me strength.

There's my niece Connie and her husband, Ochmen Murray, who had lived with me when they moved to Columbus. Connie is the daughter of my brother, George, who still resides in Upstate New York. Anyway, Connie, with her squeaky voice, and Ochmen, with his smooth baritone, would tell me over and over, "You're going to make it uncle." They would let me know that their children were pulling for me. I had tried to be the uncle that they could depend on, and now I was depending on their love. The ripples widened.

There were aunties on my father's side of the family who strengthened me. Somehow their phone calls got through and they told people to put the phone to my ears and even though I could not talk, I heard their voices and could clearly discern their West Indian/New York accents. Nearly 90-year-old Aunt Elaine would say, "My darling, you are going to make it, you are going to make it. I am praying for you." And there was Aunt Ela, who resembles my father, who insisted, "I got the prayer band at my church, and they are praying for you. I want you to know there is a Deacon here who is just waiting to meet you. You're going to make it. I do not care what the doctors say." And I don't want to forget Aunt Helen, the most emotionally frail of all of my aunties, who would call me faithfully, saying, "Johannes, I just need to know the story. I need to know that you are going to make it. I want you to know that I am praying for you." And even though I could not say a word, could not talk back to them, whenever their calls would come through, somebody would hold the phone to my ear just so I could hear them.

The calls went on day in and day out. Whether they where wheeling me into surgery or wheeling me out from surgery, there was always somebody from the family that was in the room, somebody from the family that was around me, and they never left me alone. Whenever a car was coming from Columbus to Dayton, the one constant figure that I have not talked about was my mother, Shirley E. Christian, the evangelist, the mother, the postal worker, and the one that worked for the President, as she would say, because she was a government worker. She did not care who was in the room. She just came and took her position by the left side of my bed, did not care what operation they had just done. She would find my hand, pull it out from under the blanket and just sit there and rub it. She did not talk very much any more because of her strokes. She did not try to say that much because she figured, at 80-plus years old, there was not all that much she had to say anymore. She would just sit there and rock in that chair and pray, and all I can remember her saying was that, "You are going to make it."

How could I not make it with so many people parading through the room, all telling me and telling God that I was going to make it? I am sure that I was making it because of their strength, the real will for me to live, their belief in the fact that God was able to sustain me despite all of the physical damage that had been done to my frail, weak body. They left me with no other alternative but to have a will and desire to live, as well as the strength to fight even through the darkness of this round-the-clock nightmare. I must say that it was the unrelenting love of my family that pulled me through the darkest days of my life. There were other family members whose names I have not called to this point and not because they were not present and not because their experiences were not important to me. My brother George, who I mentioned earlier, drove straight through from Upstate New York to Columbus, and then came and sat by my bed, his emotions getting the best of him. I remember my nephew, Derrick, and niece, Adrienne, providing so much support. I will forever remain in Adrienne's debt, not so much for any emotional currency, but for the constant love that she showed me not only during the time of my hospitalization but the dramatic way in which she shared time with me in my recuperation at home. There are many, many other members of our family who throughout the time of my recovery, through either phone calls or cards or money and time also heralded me to a speedy recovery.

I am told that the extent of the images that we will talk about in another chapter through an understanding of what Dr. Schmidt was able to repair, that my recovery was probably much swifter than that of most patients that he had seen with the type of injuries that I had incurred. I only wish that time and my finite brain would allow me to be sure to call the name or write the name of every person that impacted my life and the speedy recovery that I experienced. I would say at this point if you are a part of the Christian/Ellis family and extended family, then your name is included in the writing of this book and you can hold a part of the responsibility in my recovery either because of your faith, your concern or your unending love that you have expressed to me as either an uncle or friend or just a relative.

During my recovery there are several individuals outside my Christian family that have left an indelible mark in my memory. My best friend and brother in ministry, the Rev. Dr. Sheldon E. Williams and his wife, Marilyn, and their son, Emery, whom from the date of my accident until present have continued to be a friend and a brother and sister to me as have been the members of the Co-Op City Baptist Church in New York City, through their prayerful support, through their personal visits and continued telephone calls and continued love relationship that we have been able to have from prior to the accident to this present day and time. I share no closer relationship and human bond that I do with Sheldon and Marilyn Williams. I am grateful to God for their work and encouragement both personally and via telephone, and through offerings that have been sent to me through the Co-Op City Baptist Church. I must point out that it was at Co-Op City, where I ministered for the first time outside of Columbus after my accident. I am so grateful for not only his prayers but also his constant words of encouragement that I would make it and that somehow God would make a great success of my life even through such a tragic event. I am so grateful to Sheldon for not only having stood by me through my recovery, but also for joining me on my very first missionary journey to Africa in 2003. Realize at this point in time we are talking about my feelings and the people who helped to pull me through. I thank Sheldon and Marilyn for strength as we talked on the phone and as I would share my deep concerns over not being able to see or smell, or for sometimes feeling overwhelmed and confused about where I must go in life. They always told me how well I was doing and how much better I seemed to be every time we talked. Their words meant so much to me and have been so much of an encouragement to me that I do not think that I could ever repay them or help them to understand how special they are to me. For every airplane trip that Sheldon took from New York to Columbus just to be with me, either to be in ministry or just to visit me at home, I want to say "thank you," and to let you know that it was through your friendship and brotherhood that I received great strength and consolation.

My thanks and gratitude is also extended to Bishop Frederick Marshall, who has proved to be both a mentor and a father image to me in ministry, who stood by my bed and my family throughout my recovery, who raised thousands and thousands of dollars from so many places that I do not even know about to make sure that my life went without want. It was Bishop Marshall who continued to encourage me to stay in ministry, who continued to encourage me to be the man that God had called me to be, and who continued to pray with me that God would be victorious in the situation. As I look back now, I trust I gave God nothing to be displeased with even as I dealt with my anger and pain, and even the act of forgiving. Many times it was Bishop Marshall that spoke as a drum major of God in my hospital room, as well as in the nursing home, as well as in my home. He sounded a clarion call that God would stay impacted upon my life, written not only on my mind but the walls of my heart. He asked that I be granted God's strength and mercy throughout the healing process and that I emerge victorious from what are the darkest days of my life. I also wish to thank First Lady Molly Marshall, who was my friend before the accident and who remains my friend today, and a source of great inspiration and hope in my life. I am so grateful that even throughout my blindness, I have been able to share my love for them with floral designs and arrangements for both their homes as well as for their persons to bear throughout their pastoral anniversary celebrations. As Bishop Marshall would say, our relationship is only because of the Grace of God. And so it is by the Grace of God that I remained his son in ministry. His strength and unwavering belief in my recovery and me was evident by the ministers he sent to my church, Adoration and Peace Baptist Church, during my absence. He also was there personally for my members, and continued to encourage them to keep me as pastor. He remained available to my children to aid their journey of faith. I wish to thank Bishop Marshall's church, Symrna Baptist Church, as well as the Free Gospel Fellowship International, for their love and support. I thank God for all that our churches have done from around the world with their prayerful support for me as an individual, as well as the personal touches that many of our ministers have exhibited both in gifts, in visits, phone calls and words of encouragement. As I continue to pray for each of your ministries, I realize that I am only here as the result of the life and efforts of so many individuals from across this great continent and world.

The Reverend Charles E. Booth, who is known as the Renown Pulpitry of these United States, I truly thank God for what you have done and the impact that you have made upon my life. I thank God for your constant words of encouragement every time that we were able to talk on the telephone, for the uncle that you have continued to be for my children, and the guiding image of faith you are to my sisters and brothers. Our relationship has been so much more than just gifts of money or material things, because from you we reap much strength and power. My family has hung on the words of your sermons from your pulpit as well as from your tape ministry. We thank you. I have gleaned from such strong men of God. It often seems to be a wonder to me as to why God has allowed me to know such great giants as these two men.

To the Mount Olivet Baptist Church family who continued not only through my stay in Dayton, through the visits of people such as Trustee Angela Cornilus, director of the Project Linden Drug and Alcohol Counseling Agency in Columbus, Ohio, and Deacon Hugh Black, who has been my friend since 1985, who would constantly and untiringly drive back and forth between Columbus and Dayton just to stand by my side even when I could not talk. You were there for me and stood in the stead of your great pastor. To Brother Bob Easley, who has been my friend and brother from my times and days at the Mount Olivet Baptist Church, when I served as a member of the brotherhood there. I thank God for you and your prayers as well.

To Walter Toraine, who is one of the administrators of the Franklin County Children Services in Columbus, Ohio, who has been such a spiritual pillar for me, one who has shared the Jebaz prayer that God would not only feed me but enlarge my territory, who would come and spend his lunch hour with me so that I might zap from him the strength just to make it through another day. Walter, I thank God for you and for your wife and your family who allowed you to spend time with me at both the hospital and nursing home that I might recover and acts of kindness that you continue to express to me to my sisters at the Mount Olivet Baptist Church.

While there are yet many, many ministers who helped to raise money to make sure that my life would not feel the impact of being jobless and so that I would not return home to be homeless, I thank God for Bishop Andy C. Lewter. Thank you, Bishop Lewter for allowing the Columbus, Ohio community to host a city-wide benefit on my behalf at the Oakley Baptist Church, who participated in making sure that I understood the depth and breath of the love that God would allow me to experience from every facet of the City of Columbus from the mayor, to state senators, to the governor, to just common people that would stop when they see me in the street, I say thank you.

There are ministers that to me in life and, as a man of God, I have met many across this great country, but during my recovery there were two brothers in ministry that, to be honest, I never expected to see. I am so grateful for Rev. G. Tommy Turner of the Friendship Baptist Church of Columbus, Ohio, who visited me on the first Christmas Eve of the year of my accident in my living room. He had never been in my home before. We had never spent that many hours together in ministry or as colleagues, yet I had always had a great deal of respect and love for him as a man of God. I will never forget the Christmas present that he and his church family sent to me. The monetary amount does not need to be disclosed, but I thank God for the leadership that you allowed God give you, as you became a blessing to me and my family. I do not think you will ever know what your visit meant to me as a man of God. To the Rev. C. Dexter Wise, and for all of these ministers whose names I have called, most of whom I viewed to be far greater in ministry and far more prestigious than a poor country boy such as myself. That I received a visit from you at my bedside in my nursing home stay, have been able to grace your pulpit and to speak to your congregations, I feel you will never fully understand God used you to continue to lift and inspire this blind man of God.

There is one minister who, as I bring this chapter to a close, I would be so remiss if I did not give her a special place by herself, and that would be the person of the Elder Helen Jean Stewart who has been a friend, a confidante, a sister in ministry through the Interdenominational Ministerial Alliance of Columbus and vicinity, and who has been a prayer partner for almost a decade. We have prayed together on the telephone every Sunday morning, and you have joined me in prayer for such great men as the Bishop Paul S. Morton, the Bishop Larry Donnell Trotter, the Rev. Charles E. Booth, the Rev. Dr. Sheldon E. Williams, Rev. Benson, the Bishop James B. F. Roary, and Elder Bey. I thank God for Elder Stewart for her weekly visit to me in the hospital; your presence was a blessing for which I have no description, except to say that week after week you comforted me just by being there.

My fondness for Elder Stewart is extended as well to Mother Ellen Barksdale of the Shiloh Baptist Church in Columbus, Ohio, whose name I would raise at the same time because these two women are both elderly, over seventy in each case, yet they came week after week to visit with me and pray with me. I am so grateful to God for the words of Elder Stewart as she leaned over in my bed and said, "This is not sickness unto death." I think that was God's way of telling me that at some point I needed to pick up my bed and walk. Not only do I thank God for her tireless visits to the hospital, but I thank God for these two women of prayer, that they would pray in that room and pray out of that room, and pray for my constant healing, as did many hundreds of people around the world. I am sure, but these were prayers and words that I was able to hear, even when I could not respond to them. So I thank God for her and for Mother Ellen Barksdale and for the strength, which I have gleaned from them.

I believe recovery for me is not just the fact that I am alive, not just the fact that through medical science my body has been restored, but recovery for me is that fact that I have emotionally and spiritually stayed connected. God has blessed my life, that He has taken me from being a person of meager means to being a man that is unspeakably wealthy in the spirit realm. I truly believe that through the recovery process, and through what I have gleaned with my friends and family, I have become very rich and powerful in the spirit realm. The gifts given to me by the love and expressions of concern and care from so many people make it unthinkable that I could go throughout the rest of my life without giving endlessly of myself to those that I would come in contact with that have a need that could be met from my life. So as I bring this section to a close, I do so with full knowledge that the healing process, the healing virtue that has been extended to me from God is a direct result of the lives, which have touched my life. It also comes with an understanding that I must repay with fervor and tenacity the debts I owe no matter where the Lord leads my ministry. I hope that I may be a beacon of change in the lives of others, who may extract from me nuggets of faith, hope and an unwavering, undying love that is given to us by the Grace of God.

(Copy of the fourth letter Rev. Christian wrote to Jacob McNary in prison.)

Reverend Dr. Johannes J. Christian
691 Lilley Avenue
Columbus, Ohio 43205

December 4, 2004

Grace and Peace be unto you from God our Father and the Lord Jesus Christ.

I pray that all is well with you and your family at this time. I continue to pray that God our father will strengthen you. How are your studies going? What subjects are you taking? What other activities are you involved in? I know that you have figured out the importance of staying in the Word and staying prayed up. So where are you at in your Bible study? Is there a prayer group that you are a part of?

I know that I am asking allot of questions and I hope that you don't mind. I really want you to be encouraged and to find some meaningful ways to fill up your time. I know how easy it is to get discouraged or depressed. When I do not hear from you I think that's what is going on with you. If that is the case I hope that you will find some comfort in these words. The word of God says, "Lift up your head, O ye gates, and be ye lifted up ye everlasting arms and the King of Glory will come in." Who is the King of Glory? The lord strong and mighty he is the king of glory.

God wants you to look up toward him and give him all the glory with your life. So, my son, with your head lifted up and words of praise on your lips and a smile on your face go on and meet the challenges of today and every day. When you write back please tell me if it is working for you.

I hope that you will have the time to write soon. Please keep me in your prayers.

Grace and peace,

Johannes J. Christian

> "And by him all that believe
> are justified from all things ...."
>
> *- Acts 13:39*

First Steps

I am a caregiver at heart, which is why it has been so difficult for me to be the one that requires any amount of care, let alone constant care. That is why I consider it a blessing to have been able to resume my duties as an alternate caregiver for children in need.

Since the mid-1980s, more than 40 children have come to me for foster care, and it has been my sincere pleasure to provide them with a place where they could find emotional healing, love, guidance and support.

I am grateful to God that my accident did not render me unable to be a caregiver, to be a someone who is able to express and give love to such fragile individuals as these angels with whom God has blessed my home.

Due to the nature in which these special individuals have come under my care, I want to take care in discussing them because of the legal and personal responsibilities I have as a registered caregiver with the State of Ohio and the various agencies with which I am associated.

Where do I begin?

I cannot express the appreciation and gratitude I have for Mr. Christopher Kelly, executive director of Youth Advocate Services, and his staff, who greatly encouraged me to resume my efforts as foster parent as soon as I was able to return to my house after months of recovery and rehabilitation. You see I was fully prepared to give up this aspect of my life due to my blindness and plethora of ongoing medical challenges. For one, I still had a tracheotomy and had only recently come off a feeding tube. I also was still extremely sore, and was consumed with learning my surroundings as a newly sightless individual.

Mr. Kelly's words comforted and encouraged me. "Doc, you are too fine and too great a foster parent to no longer be involved with children. And whatever it takes, whatever is necessary for you to remain a foster parent, I want you to understand that we will make that commitment to you."

Wow! I replied that I did not even know if I could get a license to be a foster parent at this stage of my life, with the copious challenges I faced for an unforeseeable future?

"For them to reject you because of your disability would be against the law," Mr. Kelly countered, adding that not only would I have grounds to sue, but he would have to sue them on my behalf if the state rejected my application.

With those words, my treatment foster home essentially was back in business, so to speak. It was like I really did not miss a beat as members of our support group would come and drive me to meetings and to the classes we are required to take as foster parents in for the Franklin County agency based in Columbus, Ohio.

Meanwhile, Doreas Porter and Heidi Evans of Youth Advocate Services screened files of children in need, trying to find an appropriate child to place in my home, given my unique situation. Then one day my telephone rang and it was Heidi Evans, saying she and Doreas believe they found the perfect match for my home. I will never forget that I laughed, which is the only response I could muster immediately because I was still wearing a trach and could not talk without putting my finger over the hole in my throat.

I remember replying, "Yeah, sure. This is probably be Jack The Ripper's son, or one of the mobster's gang, or let me guess, it's somebody who has been out on the street corner selling cocaine, and you just want to find a place for them to live."

It was sour humor, but I knew they could take it, as we've known one another for many years and survived the various battles of foster care. And while biting, the commentary was not far from the truth, as most of the youths that would come to my home were very, very troubled. Before my accident, I had a reputation for taking on children no one else wanted, or could not deal with, and I had always enjoyed the challenge. It seemed that the more they had in their past and the bigger their file, the more eager I was to work with them. If they had been in juvenile detention and had been before a couple of judges, then that meant that they were good candidates for my home.

However, at this particular point in my life I did not think that those were exactly the young people I should deal with because I was extremely vulnerable and could no longer see the shenanigans that these youths were capable of engaging. I knew I needed a different kind of youth. I needed a youth that required care and love, but at the same time would be able to take on some responsibility of their own. I needed a youth that would be understanding of an individual with physical limitations, even though that individual was their care provider.

Anyway, after I relinquished the floor and stopped being cynical, Heidi Evans told me they had a young man who was originally from New York City. Well, she knew, having been a New Yorker, born and raised, and still having a heart's desire to return to New York some day, that would catch my attention. She then said that this child had been abandoned by his mother with family friends in Columbus and wound up in children's services network when they refused to care for him. The child was 15, very independent, had been responsible for helping to care for his younger siblings. In fact, he was more of a daddy to the kids than he was a sibling. They warned there might be other kinds of issues — mental health issues, perhaps — that have not been addressed at this juncture in his life. Despite his dysfunctional upbringing, the boy was a good student, who had a desire to finish school. He was well mannered, although he had a tendency toward emotional outbursts.

All in all, to me that is, this boy sounded like any other child between the ages of 13 and 18, who was coming to grips with their hormones and emotions. For those of you who are parents, I do not have to tell you what kids are capable of doing as adolescence. But this child sounded like someone I could work with, and relate to. Suddenly, I was hit with a question that stunned me given everything I've experienced of late, and the fact that it was the criminal acts of another 15-year-old who put me in this place: "Well, would you like us to bring him over so he can have a look at you and you can have a look at him?" There was a long pause on my end of the telephone.

I thought, "Johannes, are you really ready for this?" Then I thought about the fact that youth have been a continual part my adult life. I not only raised my children, but everybody else's children it seems, including nephews and nieces, and others who came to me from the streets. I truly thought that I would never be able to do that again after everything I've been through since that fateful night of July 9, 2001. Again, there was a long pause before I finally replied, "Well, yes, you can bring him over, but I want you to understand that there is no guarantee I am going to like him, there is no guarantee that I am going to say that this is going to work. It is just an opportunity to meet him and for him to meet me."

The entourage that graced my door the following day included the young man in question, his caseworker from the county office, and Heidi Evans. The child was quiet, but I sensed he was a large, and that frightened me a bit. This was weird. I realized that I couldn't see what he looked like. To get to know him, I would have to feel his face, which is a custom of many visually impaired people. I was still very awkward with feeling somebody's face and their hair to get a mental picture of what they looked like. This particular young man said he did not have a problem with be touching his face, and when I did, I got to the bottom of his ear and felt an earring. I told him I wasn't fond of earrings for men, remembering the battles I waged with my own sons regarding this issue. I remembered getting quite upset when they each went behind my back and got one. Next, I felt his hair, "Oh, God, there's a ponytail ... another no-no in my book. I began to wonder why these people were even bringing this kid to me? He appears to be somebody's hippie or some punk rocker just from the way he looked. But I did not say anything. I just kind of listened and we began to talk. He told me that he hopes one day to be a paramedic, how he planned to help save people's lives, and how he was interested in working with people, and how he liked older people. And I thought, "Wow, that's a big one. He's telling me I must be ready for the geriatrics unit."

As our meeting continued, I determined he was, in fact, a fine young man who seemed to have his head on straight. He had a great desire to finish high school, and I believe he was going to be one of the first people in his family to ever finish high school and that was really important to him. He began to share with me stories about his family, about his grandmother on his mother's side, his paternal grandfather, and another family friend who was like a grandmother to him who was Jewish. I learned he was bi-racial and that was nothing new to me, and nothing new in my family. I had bi-racial children in own family and we had bi-racial marriages throughout my family, so that was not an obstacle for me. We talked for a couple of hours and we, he and I, began sharing and speaking very honestly. I asked him how he felt being around a blind person, and it did not seem to bother him. He thought he might be able to deal with it, and I thought I might be able to try to deal with having a kid in my house again.

To be honest, there was a part of me that just looked forward to the opportunity to have a child present in my home again. I do not remember now whether I gave him an answer at that moment or whether was after a day or two. I believe I allowed them to return to their offices, and Heidi and I planned to meet again and to conduct a thorough debriefing of the situation. What I do remember was having a lot of questions for her. How would I know if I can meet his needs? How would I know if he was getting what he really needed? How could I be sure that I could get him up and get his food fixed? The people that cared for me were not supposed to cook for other people. They were there being paid to take care of me, so how could I think that I could take care of somebody else if I needed someone to take care of me? And so there were a range of questions that I had to deal with. And one by one we tried to come up with answers but most of all, I think the concern was, was this going to be a good match? Would he make it in my home? Would I make it with him? I learned the county social worker had called back and told Heidi that the young boy was really interested in living with me, and wanted to know how I felt about that? I remember saying, "Well, go ahead and let us just give it a try. But if it does not work, I need to know that you will remove him without a whole lot of hassle."

So there I was, by the grace of God, preparing to foster another blessed soul, to share the love that God had given me for children. And this young boy came into my home and two years later he left after he graduated from one of our local high schools, Walnut Ridge High School, on the far east side of Columbus. During the two years that he spent in my home, he became part of our blended family. He considered my natural children, who were much older than him, to be his brothers and sisters. They dealt with him like anybody else. When he had a smart mouth, they smart-mouthed back to him, and vice versa. They primed him to let them know when I fell down or when I did not drink enough Ensure. They got out of him details of what kind of night I might have had, how hard I was breathing, and if I was having any problems. Despite having a spy in the house – a term I use in jest – I found myself bonding with him, and he with me. He could talk to me about his class work. He could talk to me about his girlfriends. He could talk to me about his relationship with his mother and his grandmother. I will not forget the time his birth mother was scheduled to return to Columbus for a court hearing. That night he came into my room and said, "I don't know if Mom can make it. She cannot afford to pay for a bus ticket to get here and have a place to stay, and the agency is not going to help her with a hotel. I do not know what we are going to do?"

Sensing his fear and frustration, I said, "Well, isn't there a bunk bed in your bedroom?"

And he said, "Well, yes."

And I said, "Well, why wouldn't you just let your mom stay here at our house?"

Somewhat perplexed and surprised by my comment, he said, "You would let my mother stay here at your house?"

"It's not my house," I said. "It's our house."

I sensed that my reply floored him. Not only was this unheard of for him, but for the county caseworkers as well. Yet, for me, it just seemed like the natural thing to do. How could I say I loved him and not love his family, and not provide an opportunity for him to be with his family? It was bad enough that he had been separated from his mother for three years at that juncture. Again, it just seemed like the most natural thing to do.

His mother did stay with us when she got to town, and I believe it helped their experience of bonding together. It helped them to be able to relate to each other. So we shared our home with her for a weekend and they got to the court hearing and extended his stay with me. There are more experiences with this young man that I could relate, experiences that could fill another book ... now there's another idea? The bottom line is that this young man with a disjointed past became so relaxed in my home that he just became another kid. He was very opinionated and always knew that he was right about whatever he was talking about, and he wasn't afraid to express it. He would get so excited, he would start screaming and hollering at me and I would be sitting there like, "Who do you think you are screaming at? I am not the kid next door. I am the caregiver. I am the person in charge here."

I'd tell him that I was just as ignorant to the world as he at one time, but thought I had all the answers. I told him he was just like any other child that had graced my door, which I helped raise. Then it hit me like a gale, I am back. I'm doing exactly what I was doing before, what I loved doing the most outside of preaching. I have to say that those two years with that child went by too quickly. Before I knew it, we were looking at colleges and other post-high school experiences for him to get involved. He was already working at a nursing home, already taking on more responsibilities as a young man, and before I knew it I was buying a graduation gift and getting him prepared to go out into the world on his own. If there is a downside of being a caregiver, it's the feeling of loss that bookends the excitement and satisfaction you get preparing successfully preparing a child for the real world. It was such a joy in my life to go back and forth to the school, talk to the counselors with him, yell over the phone and figure out what was going on, and what we needed to do to help him become a better young man. And here we stood at graduation, and the climax of my involvement with him. His grandmother and mother came from New York to share in celebrating that fact that he earned a high school diploma. His grandmother and I agreed to share the cost of a class ring, a talisman of his achievement, as well as the cost of clothes he would wear and the ceremony. She bought the shoes. I bought the suit, shirt and tie, and we got the sign to put out front that stated, "Hurray! Hurray! He graduates today." God, it was just such an awesome experience, something I thought I lost forever when a rock took my face, my eyesight, and my independence. But here I was, doing what I love to do. How could I not thank God for such an experience? On Sunday he would get up and go to church with me, just like my natural kids. He took part in the services just like my natural kids, and yet he gave me the chance to give back to him just my natural kids did. He always stood here with his hand out saying, I need this and I need that, and whether the agency would pay for it or not, he got it. I look back at that time and I realize that, because I had the opportunity to share love with someone else that needed it – whether it was just a place to stay or meet his emotional needs, or to be father figure to him – that it was as much a time of healing for me as it was for him. It seemed like the more I did for him, God did for me in return.

Before he left my house that spring, another young man was brought to my doorstep. This young man was well over 6-feet in height, but skinny as a rail. He was quite the musician, however, and loved to play the keyboard. Music was his refuge from the physical and emotional issues that tormented him. He just played. He even brought his keyboard to the interview. When he first came to stay with me, I purchased a set of headphones so he could hear what he was playing, and so the rest of his did not have to hear it all the time. He loved the Lord and had a church background. How ironic this was that they brought him to my house, and in our conversations I found out that his father had been a good friend of mine, and had belonged to one of our sister churches. What an emotional bonding I had with this child from the very beginning. This was a kid that I had met when he was young.

He could barely remember me, but I kind of knew who he was and I knew his family. I knew his mother. I did not understand how he could be in the situation of needing a place, but I tell you because of who he was, I was able to open my arms yet one more time. And now instead of one kid, I had two kids. How could this be? I could barely take care of myself and here I had yet another teenager living with me. It was almost like old times.

It was like having my own sons, George and Tyrone, back at home again. Now, do you think these two could get along? No, of course not. I sensed frustration from my first foster son, who expressed frustration over the fact that another child found a place in my heart. "He is bothering me. He is in my territory. He is not giving me space. How could you let somebody else come in here?" These were the things that I and other parents hear from their own children. You thought it would be different because these kids needed a place to stay, that they would be grateful they had a roof over their heads. Well, they were grateful, but it did not mean that stopped being kids. I will never forget. There was a fight one night. The room was rocking. They were shoving each other against the walls, beating each other up and here I came with my cane and stood in the door banging on the door, imploring, "Could you two pipe it down in here?"

They pleaded with me, "He won't give me this. He's using this and it's mine."

"All right, I said sternly, let's go downstairs."

We went down the stairs and sat in the living room. I think we talked from 11:30 p.m. to 2:30 a.m. I think they were so tired of hearing my mouth that they would have agreed to anything I said at that point. But it didn't matter. What mattered was we learned how to live with each other and how to love each other, and how there could be differences and we could settle them without fighting and beating each other up. Man, I felt like old times had returned. It brought the "Dad" out of me, the counselor out of me, the preacher out of me, everything out of me that I thought I had in me. I thought Satan had taken something away from me, but I found out that God had given something back to me and I was able to give it to someone else. My heart's desire was just to serve God and I knew that the way I could do that was through serving others.

We finished out that school year; both of them finished out the school year, and then in the middle of the summer they moved out of my house, one right after the other, and my home was empty again. But not for long. Not for long. In just a matter of a few days I had yet another caseworker knocking at my door, one who happened to be the very caseworker of one of the young men who was in my home at the time of my accident.

She said, "I bet you never dreamed that you would take another kid from me?"

"Well, I don't know?" I replied.

"I've got this young man who is medically fragile," she said. "He is a cancer survivor, and he is wonderful young man.

I said, "Well, if he's so wonderful, why are you bringing him to me?"

I learned that he had failed in one foster home, and could not make it where he was currently living. It seems he was opinionated and was not shy about expressing his opinions. He was considered quite the challenge.

"I thought that you said he was medically fragile?" I asked.

"He is, but he's still a teenager," she said.

They brought him over for me to meet. I felt his face. This one was 6-feet-3, and I said the group, "Can't you all find any little kids to bring to me?" It seems like they were getting taller and taller. He told me that he had had an experience with the Lord. He had had a relationship with God, and then he ended up with cancer and he began to question God about his cancer. So this is why his caseworker believed I would be the perfect match in this situation? After what I had gone through, she thought it would be good for him to be around me because my faith was so great despite all that has happened. It was like he was saying, "Boy, you really do not understand." I told him that I am still coming to grips with who I am, and why I am going through what I am going through. Between this caseworker and one of her supervisors, who happened to be one of my friends who had visited me when I was in a nursing home, they believed I would be good for this young man. I'm not sure, I thought, it feels like God is ganging up on me now.

But we continued to talk for quite a while. I remember thinking that I thought the first child was opinionated. This kid made him look like Mickey Mouse. He knew everything there was to know. He was Perry Mason and he was Johnny Cochran all rolled into one. He could file, investigate and litigate every case all by himself. Heck, he could be judge, jury and executioner, if the situation called for it. He didn't give others time or room to tell him anything. It only took a few minutes to learn that all of this was merely an emotional veneer. Beneath a forceful, boisterous exterior he was very vulnerable and very weak and very much afraid. He had made it through the cancer. The doctors told him that they got all of it, but he had great fear it would return. He was still going through the chemo, and was still running back and forth to doctors. Again, on the outside he gave the impression that he was one tough dude that would survive at all costs, but on the inside withdrew in fear each time he returned to the hospital.

To be honest, I questioned whether I could take care of him. He was so different than the two previous foster children. He required much more skilled care. The cancer affected his equilibrium. What if he fell? How would I know if he bumped his head, and if he did, was it severe? If he fell down, could I help him up? How could I help him? How could I figure out what he needed medically? This child was a challenge, but I tell you the reality of the situation was it was not that great if we put our heads together and put our minds to it. The greatest blessing was that he liked the two other boys, and did not have a father, so I got a chance to be "Daddy" once again. And now, it's 2005, almost three years later, and he too is preparing to graduate from high school, with honors, I might add. What experiences we have had together in our home. There have been birthday celebrations, homecomings and proms, and participating in the marching band. And, after having to be home-schooled for two years, he was able to spend his senior in high school with his friends. How he has changed from a know-it-all kid to a polite, reserved, conversationally adept young man, who is about the face the real world. He was accepted at an Ohio university, and will begin his studies this fall. Just the other night he expressed concerned about who he really was, and what did it mean when he left my house? Would he be able to return? Where would he go on breaks from college? Did he need to go to his mother's house, or could he come to my house? Was this really his home? He had so many questions and there was so little time to give him answers. After all, was he really going to be able to make it this year and if so, how did I know? All I could tell him was that these were the same questions that most of us had when we were about the leave home, and yes, he could always come home. And yes, he could always use my address as his last known address. And yes, we would make some kind of preparation for him to come home during Christmas and Easter breaks, but no, he could not move back here indefinitely. That was okay, because nobody else could do it. If you return, you will have to leave again.

The conversation floored me as I realized the joy that has come over my life, that I have been able to give back to others. I think it has just been in giving of myself in service, giving of myself to these young men who have come through my doors that has played the most vital role in my personal healing process. First there was one, then there was two, and then there was none, and then it was back to one again, and then I had an opportunity to watch yet another boy. They said he suffered from attention deficit, hyperactivity depression (or ADHD), and that he was Bipolar. They said that he was from an unstable family, and that he was placed in one of the other foster homes in our network, and it was not working out. I heard such horrendous stories about this child of 12. The foster mother had to call the police on more than one occasion as his behavior frightened her. He would not listen to her. He was quite outrageous and out of control, and she just could not deal with him another day. And here, they wanted to know if I would watch over him and just give that foster family respite? I thought, "How could I give her a break? How could I maintain this kid? First of all, he was younger than any kid that I had ever taken. I do not take kids that are not 15." This kid is only 12 years old and he sounds like he is totally out of control, and here is the worker standing at my door, smiling and asking, "Can I come in?" I'm like, sure, but I am really scared out of my wits that I cannot control this young man. Then he comes in. They asked me if he can have a couple days of respite. That would be three days maximum, and they would take him back home. But three days turned into a month, and we were just going to stay one day at a time. He was trying to get to know me. I was trying to get to know him. He slept in his clothes. He slept on the floor. He did not hang anything up. He cried. He screamed. He really did not act like he loved being here. He constantly complained that there was nothing to do. He ate, and he ate, and he ate some more. The caseworkers were asking me, "Well, what do you think? Do you think you can handle him?" And I was like, "I don't know. I don't know. I can't make a decision here." I prayed and I asked God to give me direction.

Another foster son was living with me as well. He had not yet graduated from high school. I knew he was suspicious of the new child. The two of them did not get along, and I did not know what to do? I was about to say, "Well, God, you have helped me this far, but this kid really seems like more of a challenge than I have been able to have so far since my accident." I was about give up. My heart was saying it was okay, but my soul told me differently. I finally reached the decision that I would try to care for him. And just when I made up my mind, the caseworker showed up and said, "Hey, another family in the network said they could take him." My burden had been lifted, as the other family took this child. It would last. Within two weeks, the caseworker was on the phone again, asking me if I'd be willing to take him again? Well, it was too late to refuse, when I only recently decided to give it a try. So they brought him back, and he finished the school year. We're now getting ready to finish our second school year together. I cannot begin to tell you the changes that I have seen come over this young man's life. Yes, he is Bi-polar. He takes three different kinds of medication three times a day. But what love I have received from a child who has never known his real father, who is not of the same race as me. I had the opportunity to baptize him as a believer.

I had the opportunity to be with him as he has gone to Boy Scouts and learned martial arts. I was with him when he was asked to take part in the 2005 Arnold Schwartzenegger Fitness Classic, a huge annual event here in Columbus. He is turning into such a responsible young man, but he still has his moments. He turned 13 and occasionally fights with me over some issue. He is not quite there yet; he argues that I need to treat him more like he is an adult. As I do it, I sense he is becoming more and more of a young man, and that truly pulls my heartstrings. I wish I could say he has been a perfect child this year, but that's not true. For this child, it's a massive step that he finished the school year attending the same school in which he started. I had to make a deal with him to be able to bring home a bicycle. I had to prime him and pump him to get his room cleaned. It seems I cannot buy enough hot potato chips for him to eat because it seems he can eat a whole case in one night. Despite ongoing challenges, I have to tell you that the love he brings to me is unsurpassable. Here is a boy that once could not look anybody in the eye, who now throws his arms around me and hug me, and who can weasel things out of me that I would not give my own kids. All he wanted was somebody to love him, and it warms my heart that he and the other two young men in my house get along and can work as a team when the need arises.

I cannot possibly tell this story without talking about the last young boy to come to my house … number five since the accident. He also is in his second year living with Johannes and friends. I will just call him "the smiler." I am told he has a killer smile. He will be 17 soon. He is a junior in high school, and carries a 4.3 grade point average on a 4-point scale. I never even knew what a 4-point was, let alone a 4.3. He is taking 18 courses.

Those are advanced college courses in high school, and people say he looks like he is really my own natural son. He has got my own winsome ways and my own corny sense of humor. And to top it off, he runs like I did when I was in high school. He was undefeated in the regular season in several events, earned a berth in the divisional track meet, and nearly made it to the state championships.

The only difference here is that I made it to the state championships when I was in high school in New York. He has another year to compete, however, and I think he'll qualify for the state championships in 2006. As you may sense, we have much in common. He loves to do crafts, and he helps me continue doing the crafts that I like to do, such as making button covers, picture frames, or floral arrangements. He seems to enjoy doing them as well. He is probably one of the most perfect young men I have ever seen in my life. He cannot do enough for me, and I cannot seem to do enough for him. I do so much for him, I hear the other one complain that I spoil him more, meaning I must be careful to maintain balance in our home. Just because people think that they are getting so much more from me, if they only knew that what these young boys have offered is much more than anybody would ever know. They have been a completion of my life; a part of my life that I thought ended after the accident. My heart's desire would be to adopt every one them and make them all Christians, and just continue to extend my family on and on and on.

I am looking forward to yet another year with this young man as he finishes out his senior year. I pray that God will keep him in my home. I pray that despite my blindness and despite my continued medical concerns, God will enable me to continue to be a father, because he, too, has never known his father and is so proud he can call me Dad, so proud when he can stand against my other five children and say, "Now, I am the sixth of five." Just one more added onto.

I am so grateful to God for the ability and the opportunity to give back to these young men that have come and graced my home with their presence, with their problems, with their concerns and their cares for in my taking them in, I have been able to give to them an unselfish love and have helped to spurn myself on to being healed. Jesus has said that by his stripes we are healed. I think that somehow his stripes have come to me through the healing of sharing my love with these who have needed it the most. I tell you that it has been caring for these young men that have made my life really worth living. Watching them interact with my grandchildren and with my natural children and be a part of my church family has given me the will and energy to be all that God would have me to be. Truly, my healing has not only been in the physical sense, my healing has come by being in the churches, providing a home and being a caregiver for them who have needed it the most.

Somewhere along the path of my healing process God also sent me three angels.

The Lord has told us to be careful how one treats strangers for some have entertained angels unaware, and in my recovery process I believe that there were three angels that have come to me, to assist me in my healing process. Angels, not in the spiritual sense, but in the physical realm. Nevertheless, I believe they are angels sent by God. The first angel I have talked about already and that would be that of **Dr. Steven Schmidt**, the plastic surgeon that was in the trauma center the night that I arrived via life-flight at the Miami Valley Medical Center. I believe I have talked about him at length as being a fine outstanding surgeon and an outstanding man of God.

In addition to Dr. Schmidt, are two other men that have been prevalent in the healing process, that have not been afraid of the physical destruction and psychological trauma I battled, particularly in the early stages my healing and path to forgiveness.

These men saved me on both the physical and emotional planes, and prevented me from withering away, which would have been so easy to do.

When I finally returned home from the nursing home I was assigned to after the hospital, I knew I was going to need homecare, or aftercare as the medical community calls it. Inquiries into such services lead me to Care Star, which is the community agency network that helps to keep people in their homes.

After determining I would be eligible for nursing care in-home, I was asked if I knew of any care providers I may engage.

I didn't but I remember a friend, George (XXXX), who had used me to care for other people in our community. And now that I was in need of care myself, I spoke with George, who said he was aware of my situation and expressed how sorry he was to hear about my visual impairment and other injures.

George and his staff assisted me in identifying a service provider that may meet my needs.

We placed a call and placed an order for a qualified caregiver. It was a few days after we had made the request that I received a phone call from the agency, telling me they had a nurse they wanted to send over for me meet. The following morning at 7 a.m. I heard a knock on the door. A tall, lanky, very dark-skinned African-American man with a great big white smile greeted me.

In a very detectable African accent, he said that his name was **Abdul Seesay**, and that he was Saddam Hussein's cousin. Stunned by his greeting, I quickly realized it was a joke when he laughed one of the most infectious laughs I had ever heard. He then said, "My name is Abdul and I am a Christian." And I said, "Oh, okay, well, come on in." At that point, I wasn't quite sure how to take him. Was he really joking the first time or the second time, I wondered? Over the course of our now multi-year relationship, I've learned that Abdul is one of the most sincere, gentle, caring men I've ever known. He immediately began to provide medical services to me by cleaning my trach, which had to be drained every morning, by taking care of the remainder of my feeding tube that was still in me, and cleaning my prosthetic eyes, which at that time were round objects without lenses inserted to make sure my sockets would not become permanently shut. He also recorded my vitals. Remember, this guy had just stopped to meet me, but within 30 minutes have given me deft, expert care.

You may be wondering how a person that just stopped by for a few minutes to take care of some mundane physical medical needs could be considered an angel? Well, I believe that God sends people into our lives to meet specific needs. Abdul is not only a wonderful nurse who received his training in the United States, but he hails from Africa. Specifically, his hometown is Freetown, in the country of Sierra Leone. He is of a humble upbringing. His father worked as a custodian in a college in his hometown, and he has many brothers and sisters. He is married to a wonderful African lady by the name of Romato, and they have two children who have adopted me as a surrogate grandfather. Abdul has become not only my caregiver; he's also become another son. We have a two-way relationship. I give to him and he gives to me. Over the course of the almost four years that he has tended to my care, he is the only nurse that I have ever had in-home. And while I am sure he has had plenty of opportunity to give me up and get another patient, he has stood in there and plugged in with me despite my sometimes nasty attitude, my grumpiness, and my depression. He has been there for me those time when it would have been easier to kill myself; not that I would, but I'll admit I've felt that way. Through it all he has maintained a positive attitude and a Christian attitude, often asking me, "Doc, what would Jesus do?" Or he'll say, "Is that how Jesus would have me react?" And he never fails to ask me, "Where is your faith and trust in God?" And yet he has the courage and sincerity to fuss at me when he felt I was not physically well enough to go to church. Appreciating his candor and concern, I would make the final decision, saying, "You know, it is my choice, and if I am too sick to go and want to go, it is my business." I will never forget one Easter Sunday morning following one of my numerous surgeries. My head was swollen like a watermelon. My eyes were puffy. My mouth was sore and I was taking pain pills every three hours, but yet I had promised myself that I was going to go to church this Easter Sunday morning. Well, dear, sweet Abdul had convinced himself that I was too sick to go, and he did everything but hide my cane that Sunday morning. He told my sons and daughters that he didn't think I was well enough to attend services. My children agreed with him, thinking I was being pig-headed to continue to insist otherwise.

After Abdul left the house, I told my son, George, to pick me up, and get me ready for church. Still blanching at the idea, I found myself making a deal with them. I told them I would not sit through the entire Easter service, but wanted to stay long enough to hear the morning message. I promised I would not stay until the end of service, and would not have a conversation with anyone. They could whisk me out before the benediction. Of course I did not mean any of that. I just really thought that if they got me there, they would see how well I was doing and let me stay. Needless to say, about halfway through service, my son did come back to the house to pick me up. I hobbled down the stairs and they had me wrapped from head to toe, including a scarf all the way around my head so that I would not get any of the cold air to become in to my face. When I got to church and got to the door of the sanctuary, everything stopped. The preacher, everyone stood up and began applauding as I walked from the back of the church to take my seat in the front row. There was total pandemonium in our congregation that day. I was allowed to spend about 15 minutes in church that Easter Sunday morning before my son stood up, approached me and said it was time to go. They put my coat on me, wrapped my head back up with a towel, everybody said goodbye, and they whizzed me out of the church before I could speak with anyone.

Later than day, when he arrived for my afternoon care, I could tell Abdul was very displeased with the decision I had made.

"You just had to have it your way," he scolded.

I looked at him and said, "I'm like Jesus. Did you not think I had to be about My Father's business?"

Abdul could only laugh, saying, "You are so hard-headed."

"I know," I said. "I'm just like my nurse."

"How so," he inquired.

"Well, you are just as hard-headed as I am," I said.

But the years, Abdul and I have had many interesting conversation. He being a foreigner and all, there are things about our culture, our government, and our race that he doesn't understand. He has asked me over and over again for advice in different situations, and I've been pleased to provide assistance, whether it be professional, financial or marital matters. I even helped him determine which school would give his children the greatest opportunities for success in life. I felt honored with he asked me to write a letter of recommendation for his daughter to be able to attend one of the Christian schools in a nearby city. Truly I thank God for this man of God that continues to be a servant to many, but most of all I am grateful to God that he has become a servant of God, His servant to me in many ways as he has continued to set out my medications, clean out my eyes, make my doctors' appointments and help to deal with my many moments of depression and fear as well with my good times and fear in my family as one of my children.

There is yet one other angel that God has sent my way. It would be Billy Adams. Mr. Billy, as I and everyone else calls him, is in his mid-70s, and is a retired executive chef, who came to me shortly after Abdul. When Billy came to me, he was told that his No. 1 job was to fatten me up. At that time I was down to about 89 pounds, and a stiff wind could have blown me over. I had no appetite, no teeth to eat with, and all of my food had to be ground up in my food processor. Just imagine it? But Billy, who enjoyed cooking to the hilt, who has always been a gentleman's gentleman, felt like this was a mission from God because he had the opportunity to take care of a man of God. He was more religious in coming to work to serve as my caretaker than some people are in going to church on Sunday morning. If there was not milk in my house, he stopped and bought milk on the way. If I thought I wanted a donut, he stopped and bought the donut. He took my clothes back and forth to the cleaners, and he washed bed sheets and clothes. He cleaned my house more immaculately than any maid service would have ever done, and he had a love for my Chihuahua-mixed dog named Hezekiah (or "Hezzie" for short). He would stand in the kitchen and carry on a conversation with Hezzie, and you would think that he was talking to another adult. I swear if you listened close enough, you'd sometimes hear Hezzie answer him. I know some of you may think that I am joking, but I can only pray that someday you will get to talk with Mr. Billy or Hezzie to find out that I am really telling the truth. I tell you, Mr. Billy worried about me like a mother worried about her chicks. If I had to go for surgery, he was there before I left for the hospital, and no matter what time I came home, he was there. If I had to take medication, he made sure that the requirements were met to get the medication. He made sure that Abdul knew everything, even if I stubbed my toe or bumped my head.

And if I did not drink enough Ensure, he wrote it down and Abdul knew that as well, and I head about it later.

As you can see, I really love both of these men and consider them angels from heaven. Even so, it doesn't mean I don't know what they're up to. They've conspired against me like a angelic tag-team to make sure I was going to get better whether I wanted to or not. Sure, I jest, but remember, I couldn't see them if they huddle in a corner somewhere and plot my survival.

Back to reality, nothing pleases Mr. Billy more than to have the opportunity to lay out my clothes. If I was going to the hospital or going to the doctor's office, the outfit I wore had to be just right. If I was going to meet the mayor or some other dignitary from, he made sure I wore my blue or my black suit. He'd select the right tie and the right handkerchief for each occasion. People thought that I was dressing myself and I never told them any different, but it was Mr. Billy who was making sure the clothes met the demand no matter how banged up I was feeling. He'd always say, "Well you don't have to go out looking raggedy just because your head looks raggedy." He had a way and he had a love for the Lord. Don't get me wrong, because we had our conflicts. Mr. Billy can argue with the best of them, and so can I. Not a day goes by that we don't engage in a verbal scuffle; it's like we needed it to breathe. After every disagreement, however, we would come to the sunshine. He would come in and say, "I'm sorry. I know I should be ... you are the boss and I shouldn't say nothing."

And then every now and then he pull the age card, saying "Well you know I am older than you so you ought to be listening to me." I did not have the heart to tell him that he had really become like a daddy to me. In so many ways, no matter what he said, I knew it always made sense, and I really needed to listen to him.

One of the saddest days in my life was when he determined that the steps in my house were too much for him to climb because of his failing health and his really bad knees. It would take him a long time to climb up my stairs in the morning to see if I was alive and to make up my bed, and by the time he would get there, he would have tears running down his face because his knees hurt so bad. I tried to lighten his work up so that he would only have to cook in the downstairs and allow somebody else to clean. But he said he just did not feel comfortable because he did not feel like he could meet all of my needs. We knew then it was really time for him to retire. But just a note that even though Mr. Billy retired from service, he did not retire from friendship and he never retired from being my surrogate father. Long after his retirement, I still go to my phone when it is ringing and hear a voice on the other end saying, "Man, whatcha' you doing? How's Hezzie? And how are the boys?" Then he'd add, "I'm coming over soon. I'm going to make you another meal." That's the voice of my angel, Mr. Billy.

I tell you often in life you meet many people. In scripture we are told to be careful of how we entertain strangers because some have entertained angels unaware. I believe that God was speaking to me.

Little did I know that through the course of such accident that God would bring to me such vibrant, caring angels that would hover over me, that would attend to my medical, my physical, my emotional, and my spiritual needs to be met by such mighty, mighty men of God.

This chapter is intended to serve as a meager tribute to them, and to let them know how much I care because God knows I don't always voice it as much as I should. May God bless and keep all of you always.

(Author's note: The following is a Letter-to-the-Editor written by a Trotwood, Ohio woman following a published update on Dr. Christian's healing process in early 2005.)

Story perfect for Easter

Date: April 3, 2005
Publication: *Dayton Daily News* (OH)
Section: Opinion
Page: B7

Re "The power of forgiveness," March 27: What a living saint the Rev. Johannes Christian is. As I read the article in Easter Sunday's paper, tears rolled down my face. If he can forgive the boy who did this to him, then any of us can, and should, forgive anyone who offends us.

Christian (what an appropriate name) is certainly an inspiration to all of us.

And now the young man responsible for his being blinded wants to become a Christian songwriter. Miracles never cease.

That is a perfect story to feature on Easter.

JEAN RYAN

Trotwood (OH)

> "In whom we have redemption through his blood, the forgiveness of sins, according to the riches of his grace ...."
>
> - Ephesians 1:7

Future Steps

Scripture tell us, "To whom much is given, much is required." I truly believe God has been gracious in extending his grace and mercy to me. Much has been given to me. The extension of my life is, I believe, God's unmerited favor of grace and mercy.

Truly I could have died that night I was struck by a rock, but God has seen fit to give me a second chance on life. Anyone who knows God understands it is not beyond the realm of possibility that he is a God of a second chances. Throughout scripture we see evidence where God extends a hand of grace and mercy in allowing individuals another opportunity to redeem themselves or to continue to do His will.

So it is with my life. I believe that the extension of my life has been given to me with yet another purpose. While I believe that I have been called since I was a young boy into to the ministry and given many opportunities to spread the gospel message on the East Coast as well as in the Midwest and in other parts of the United States, I believe that God was yet and still pruning me and preparing me for yet a greater mission. During my recovery process, as I traveled back and forth to the Miami Valley Hospital and to Centerville, Ohio, which is where Dr.

Steven Schmidt, my plastic surgeon, had his practice, I believe that God had enabled me to establish a relationship with yet another man of God in the person of Dr. Steven Schmidt. He is much more than just a plastic surgeon, but a husband and father, and a deeply devout Christian, very active in his religious affiliation with the Seven Day Adventist Church. He is a product of a missionary's daughter and the grandson of a missionary who had spent some time in the Philippines and in the Central America region. The adage that "apples don't fall far from the tree" would be very apropos in his life in that as his grandfather was a missionary and his mother was the product of a missionary, some of that fervor for missions has truly been spawned into his life. While he's a terrific plastic surgeon, he still has a desire to be able to serve others. So in the spring of 2003, Dr. Schmidt, while preparing me for yet another surgery, made me aware of the fact that he had been given an opportunity to accompany another doctor to Central America to the country of Guatemala. There he would be taking the opportunity to do surgery on children that had been born with cleft palates and hair lips, and that this was going to be a mission trip, an opportunity for him to give back in service to the God that had been so gracious to him. It would be an opportunity for Dr. Schmidt to continue the kind of mission work that his grandfather had done and that his mother, who was a nurse in her own right, had grown up being a part of. In some ways I think that if Dr. Schmidt could be a full time missionary doing this 365 days a year, that it would be a great reward for him and a great satisfaction. Howbeit that life has caused him to have a wonderful practice, so this would be the first time that he would have the opportunity to travel to Central America and to give back some of the gifts that God had given him in the way of missions to these children and families that would have otherwise not been able to afford such surgery.

I'll never forget, as we sat in his office that day and he was checking the repairs on my mouth and trying to determine how to yet tweak the wonderful medical job that he had already done, he looked at me, as though I could have

looked into his eyes, and said, "Well, how would you like to take a trip to Central America with me? I'm going there on a mission trip." I think it was more in jest, because I don't believe that I really thought that I was anywhere near ready for a trip outside of the country in terms of how far I had come in the healing process. I believe at that point we were still trying to determine how to remove some of the scar tissue from my forehead where we had done the skin grafting some months previously. The skin graft healed, but it left some discoloration and the discoloration went across the entirety of my forehead from left to right, with about an inch and a half width across the top of my forehead. It was very noticeable and I'm told it looked something like a burn, or the scarring that someone might have had from a burn. During this visit we were determining how he would put implants in the top of my head underneath the skin, and the stretch the skin weekly by putting a saline solution inside of the implants. This would give the skin an opportunity to stretch and after we had stretched it enough, he would take the then stretched skin and pull it upwards towards the top of my scalp. This would give me a fresh skin and give him the opportunity to cut out the scar tissue that was covering the forehead. This was to be a rather lengthy project and as we started it in the spring of the year, it would be some six weeks constantly traveling back and forth from Columbus to his office in Centerville.

As we were in conversation, he was really excited about this opportunity to go to Central America and it became very apparent to me that he truly wanted me to accompany him. One of the things I think people really didn't realize was how much Dr. Schmidt and I have in common, and that is the fact that both of us, even though we are each doctors in our own rights and people take us to be very serious people on the outside, I think both of us are pretty overgrown kids. We both get really excited about the opportunity to be used by God and the opportunity to serve others. So he kind of had that winsome grin on his face and kind of smiling, and just had a kind of giddy attitude that he was going to have an opportunity to be used by God in an area where he had not been used before. As we talked, he assured me that even having the implant in my head, it wouldn't be impossibility for me to accompany him on such a trip. We talked about the feasibility of expanding the implants while they were still in my head while we were in Central America, that we could find a spot and he'd be able to just add the saline solution at the appropriate time as if we were still in the States. It gave me plenty of food for thought. Obviously the opportunity was there for me to accompany him. The desire was there for me to go, and he was more than happy for me to accompany him and the team of people making the mission.

As I sat in his chair that day, I truly had the heart to go and the desire to go, and in my mind I realized that I really did not have the finances to go. I was barely making it on the money that I was getting from my Social Security Disability and pretty much exhausted any bank savings and gifts that I had been given over the two years of my recovery. But the opportunity to go to Guatemala was obviously there and as Dr. Schmidt and I talked I didn't really share that part with him, but I did share that there was an interest. I could really feel the moving of the Holy Spirit in my heart that this would be a wonderful opportunity to go partially across the world and being able to share the wonderful experience that God had given me in being able to forgive Jacob for his deeds and his part in my accident. It was also an opportunity for me to be able to share with others of a different nationality, different culture, different part of the world, how wonderful God had been to me in extending my life and how wonderful He had been to me through the healing process; that even though I didn't have my eyes, that things were not any worse than they were.

I returned home that day excited in my spirit about the possibilities of going to Guatemala and realizing that there was still monumental tasks of things that I needed to do to be able to go. First, would who would go with me, and second, how would we pay for such a trip? I always thought that missions took an exorbitant amount of money. I thought it would cost thousands and thousands of dollars to go to Guatemala from Columbus, Ohio. I believe the city that where Dr. Schmidt was going was somewhere near Antigua, and that he would be working with another plastic surgeon in that area.

That day I sat in my room at home and began to pray and in the spirit began to ask God to really direct me. Again, I thought about who would travel with me, and how would we foot the bill? My church, Adoration and Peace Baptist Church, was in no financial position to pay for such a mission trip. We have a small congregation, and the church doesn't pay me to be its pastor. Most of the time, 80 percent pf the offering at that point was probably my offering, my tithe to God, and that pretty much went to keep the church stable in terms of paying for the needs of our local congregation. But, nevertheless, I put it up before the Lord that if this was something that He wanted me to do that, first of all, I was willing to go and be a witness for Him, and that I would allow Him to use me in whatever way He saw to use me. As I prepared in my spirit to go, I began to ask God who would go with me.

At that point a minister at our church, Ray Moss, who had been very active in the congregation, showed some interest as I shared with the congregation that Sunday that there was an opportunity to go to Guatemala with my plastic surgeon. Ray, who had been working off and on throughout his life, just happened to be working at that point through an agency where he did telephone sales. Ray was actually a very good person as a telephone solicitor. He was doing a great job renewing people with their magazine subscriptions and was making a pretty decent amount of money in addition to what he received from Social Security. He was probably doing better than he had done in previous years.

Ray said he was very interested in going on such a mission trip and shared with me over and over about his missions that he had done through some of the Christian relief organizations in sponsoring children around the world, especially in Africa and South America. Ray continued to show much interest and understood that he would need to pay his own way, would have to assist me with day-to-day needs, and keep an eye on me.

As we began to share with our congregation our plan, I'll never forget how several of the women – especially Mother Hattie and Mother Anna Anderson – practically delivered an ultimatum to Ray, saying, "If you take our pastor half way around the world, we're holding you responsible for making sure that you bring him back safe and sound and in the same condition that he left here in." Now Ray, who is 6-feet-3 and was more than 250 pounds at the time, did not question their resolve, knowing these frail senior citizens would keep their word if anything happened to their pastor. Nevertheless, Ray maintained that he was interested, and I assured him as the information about Guatemala came to me, I would share it with him.

The trip to Guatemala wasn't as expensive as I thought it would be. I got a phone call one afternoon from Dr. Schmidt's office, saying that they were ready to buy the airplane tickets. The tickets came to around $460 each, which really was quite modest for being able to fly that far. Ray and I purchased our tickets, meaning we cleared the first hurdle of our mission trip.

Next, we realized we would need passports. Since neither of us ever had a passport, we went downtown to find the applications for passports. First we went to the Post Office in our local community, only to find out that in the ghetto, they don't carry such applications for passports.

So we went to the main Columbus Post office, where we were told we could get the necessary applications. Next we needed to get copies of our birth certificate and state I.D.s and we did that in the downtown area. Then we began to make some phone calls, because we realized we didn't have a lot of time between when we were ordering these passports and the time it would take for them to be turned around. We spoke with an assistant to U.S. Sen. John Glenn, who gave us the name of some individuals in the Immigration Office in New Orleans, who may be able to help us expedite our passports. So Ray and I filled out the information, drove to a local Kinko's store, had the appropriate photographs taken, compiled the information and drove back to the Post Office to send everything in the overnight mail. The gentleman behind the counter at the Post Office was nearly as excited about our going as we were, after we explained the reason we were trying to expedite the process. Our hearts were filled with excitement as we jumped over the various hurdles that were placed before us.

After we mailed the Passport applications, we call the individual in New Orleans whose name we had been given, and were assured that he would hand carry our applications through the process.

After applying for our passports, we spent another morning on the telephone finding out where we needed to go to get vaccinations in order to travel to Guatemala. At that point both Ray and I learned that each of us had no great love for shots, but both of us were willing to hold each other's hands as we got stuck as many times as we might need to get stuck to go on this trip. We made several calls and found out Ohio State University Hospitals had an overseas clinic where they give shots. We also learned the shots would cost us almost $200 each, a price tag we both considered steep given our modest incomes.

So, we continued our search, contacting the county office to find out if they offered any overseas shots. We learned that if we went to the health clinic for the City of Columbus, that they had an overseas clinic and their shots were somewhere between $30 and $60. We also learned that the Web site for the Center for Disease Control's would tell us what shots were mandatory and what shots were suggested. We met a wonderful nurse at the Columbus City Health Clinic who was very, very helpful. She recanted the same shots that were listed on the CDC's Web site, and assisted us in filling out the necessary information cards.

After going downtown and filling out the cards, we realized that we needed to come back for a second round of shots. At such time Ray would go ahead of me and then I would have my aid take me down and finish that process.

So we had an interest in going, our passports were ordered and our vaccination process was underway. We learned, however, there was still one more shot that was required for overseas travel, and that was to protect us against malaria. It was not really a shot, but one more prescription that was necessary. Dr. Schmidt was gracious enough to write the prescription for that and we were able to get that filled. I went over that with my nurse, Abdul Seesay, who came to my house daily. We looked at the timeline to start administering the antidote for the malaria. Having done that, we now had everything in place that we needed to have for the trip.

We realized it was going to take a few days for the passports to get back to us, and during that time we had a few other things to take care of. I was constantly keeping the church updated Sunday mornings as to how we were progressing on. We had several people who were praying with us that our passports would get back here in time.

While waiting for our passports, I received a call from Dr. Schmidt, who said they were ready to order our airplane tickets. The tickets were going to take about half of one of my Social Security Disability checks, but it was going to be well worth it as far as I was concerned. It was towards the end of the month when the tickets needed to be paid for and we were using my Visa debit card as a credit card. I remember giving it to the brother over the telephone and he was willing to order our tickets with Dr. Schmidt and the rest of the team.

Then I got confirmation that the tickets had been paid for. There was such a joy inside of me, such an extension of who I am and the opportunity to be prepared to go minister halfway around the world. I didn't know what I was going to be doing on the mission trip other than talking, and wasn't sure who I would be talking to or who would be interested in my story, but I was being told that somebody would be. God was gracious and yet this opportunity was being extended to us.

A few weeks passed without word about our passports. Then, one day, Ray called me and in excited tones said, "Doc, we've got a package." He opened it and sure enough there was his passport. It had come in a regular envelope even though we had sent a special delivery envelope to mail the two passports back to us. Even though the applications had gone out together, he had received his at his home in return mail in a plain envelope. He was so excited. I went to the mailbox that morning to see if I had received mine, but there was no special delivery and definitely no passport. That was day one. We waited, day two, but still I did not get a passport in the mail. About three days later I got my special delivery package with my passport in it – three days after Ray received his via regular mail. I wondered about all the extra money I paid to have the special delivery? Needless to say, we both had our passports, and in plenty of time to make the trip. The next thing we did is prepare to travel to Central America, a place neither of us had ever been. We were excited and apprehensive all at once. What we did know was that we had a wonderful opportunity to go and be used by God, with a medical team that was preparing to go. Little did we know, but it was the first time for most of us to be going on such a trip. So we were all trying to prepare in whatever way we could.

Ray and I had a list of things that we wanted to accomplish, and one was that we wanted to take Bibles with us. So we made phone calls to the American Bible Society, trying to line up Bibles that we could find in Spanish. We were in the south end of Columbus going through a Dollar General store, when Ray stumbled onto some cases of Bibles. A sign on the box indicated that each Bible cost $1. We purchased four cases of Bibles that day. We decided to take two cases with us, and give two cases to our congregation. We also tried to find clothing that we wanted to distribute to children we would meet in Guatemala. We determined that we would pack two suitcases: one suitcase would have our clothes; the other suitcase would be the stuff that we would give away. Our trip inventory included Bibles and other books, tapes, socks, clothes and other items that people from the church put together, including bags of toothpaste, combs, brushes, and other toiletry items. This was the beginning of a mission project and, for me; missions just meant the opportunity to extend myself outside of my normal routine. Going to Guatemala was going to be doing just that.

I'm embarrassed to say that I really didn't know where Guatemala was located within Central America, so Ray and I consulted a map and the Internet to learn more. We learned that majority of those living in Guatemala were of Mayan descent, and that most spoke a form of Spanish. The information helped us prepare. We knew it was going to be a hot place, warmer than where we were. My assistant was in charge of helping us figure out what it was that I would wear so that I could look like a preacher and still be cool enough to minister. Then I wondered about a lack of particulars. Where would I preach? Are their churches where we're going? Dr. Schmidt assisted me by making contact with several individuals in Antigua. He made contact with a minister from the Christian Missionary Alliance Church, who set up preaching opportunities for me.

While this was Dr. Schmidt's first time on a mission trip, we learned that the mission project actually had been going on for a number of years, that a Dr. Wilson had been down to Guatemala probably some 10 to 12 times and was really looking to hand over the opportunity for this trip to be headed up by a younger doctor since he was getting ready to retire. He, as God would have it, would be trying to hand this over to Dr. Schmidt, which he did not know at that time. In hindsight, if you look at how the particulars of this mission came together, you can see God's hand guiding our efforts.

There was another young pastor in the Dayton area that was kind of helping to coordinate ordering the tickets and getting things lined up for the trip. He was the person that we had given our information to with our visas to purchase our tickets. He was also the one making the contact with the Christian Missionary Alliance Churches in the Guatemalan area. He would identify the individual that we would make contact with would be the superintendent or a district area representative in the Guatemala area for us.

So the day arrived when we were to leave for Guatemala. We spent the night before packing. Members of our church came up with gifts and donations to make sure that we'd be able to cover our rooms using some of the money that I had received from Victims of Crime from a payment that came through just days before my departure. So the trip to Guatemala was now a reality.

As I was preparing to go, my sisters Jean and Elaine were so instrumental as they always are in my life. They came the night before to make sure everything was all packed. They were helping to take me to the airport.

So the day of our departure had finally arrived. We had an early morning flight. Arrangements had been made through Central Ohio Cab Company to transport Ray and myself to the airport. A friend who was part owner of a taxicab company came and personally took us to the airport in his Suburban wagon. He picked me up at my house and then Ray from his apartment. He took us to the airport early that morning and dropped us off. As was his custom, there was no charge for the trip to the airport, saving us $20. He said he did as a favor to us and to God. We were now ready to take flight on what was to be my very first mission trip and the very first mission trip for Ray.

On the Sunday before we left for Guatemala, one of our church members, Brother Zeta, gave the children's sermon. Zeta is originally from Eritrea, a country in East Africa. Zeta had fled his homeland during its war with neighboring Ethiopia. This particular Sunday, Zeta shared the different customs between the children of Eritrea and the children of our church. He talked about the similarities that children would have in terms of helping their parents, having the opportunity to be educated and to play with other children. As Zeta continued talking about his village of Senafe, located in southern Eritrea, near Ethiopian border, he became very sad. He discussed how the United States was country of opportunity and great wealth, and how he was fortunate to live here. But thinking about this made him sad, thinking about how children in his war-torn country go to bed hungry, and about how a severe drought forces parents to use bathing water as drinking water.

By the time Brother Zeta had finished telling his story, there wasn't a dry eye in the church. Adults were crying. Children were crying. Brother Zeta was crying. I couldn't see their tears, but I could hear the sobs. It was difficult to hear this story and not touched deeply. As a congregation, we said a prayer for the people of Eritrea, and it made me think. Mind you, my life had been changing dramatically since the accident. God had been dealing with me in many areas. This was the last Sunday before I was to leave the country to go to Guatemala on what was to be my very first foreign mission trip. In many ways I felt like the Apostle Paul. I was on my way to the other side of the world. I didn't know exactly how God wanted to use me. I just knew that I was going and wherever a person would take the time to listen, I was going to talk about forgiveness, and I was going to talk about the love of God. I was going to tell my story and tell about how God had enabled me to forgive this child of 15, who threw a rock over a bridge and the rock had gone through the windshield of my car. I was going to tell the story one more time of God's saving grace that instead of dying God had rescued my life.

I didn't quite know whom I was going to have the opportunity to tell my story to, but I believed God was preparing the ears of the people in Guatemala and Central America to hear my story. I believed that God was going to provide me an opportunity to share a story about His grace and His love with someone. I wanted to be able to tell somebody how my body had been racked with pain, but how God had healed me and brought me back to life. I wanted to be able to tell somebody that when there appeared to be no hope in the midst of having my eyes knocked, literally, out of my head, that despite the fact that I lived in what was now a very dark world, that there was light at the end of the tunnel; that Jesus who had come to be the Light of the World, was still ever-shining in my soul.

I was prepared to walk out of the door of our church and embark on a journey where I had never been before, in a part of the world where I had never gone before, with people that I really didn't know. The only people I knew were Ray, Dr. Schmidt and one of his nurses who was accompanying the team. As for Dr. Schmidt and his nurse, I really didn't know them in a personal way. My relationship was primarily that of a doctor and patient, and somewhat of being brothers in the Lord. I was preparing to journey thousands of miles to spread the word of God to people I've never met, to people I may never see again. God, what am I doing? Am I ready for such a big step?

I'm preparing to leave my congregation and travel abroad, when Brother Zeta shares a story that touches my soul. God, is this what you want from me? Our needs are so great in our backyard. Do you want me to travel abroad to do your work? First Guatemala. Is Eritrea next? And what does the future hold?

As I returned to the pulpit after Zeta's story, I stopped to let him know his message had not fallen on deaf ears, that truly it was a confession that touched my heart. I turned to him and I said, "I realize this may not seem like very much to you, but I want you to know that I'm on my way to Guatemala this week, but as soon as I return, I will be on yet another mission, for God had truly touched my heart and I realized in that moment that there really was a reason for my existence. And the scripture that said, "To whom much is given, much is required," must truly have been given to me.

I had been blessed to continue to be a pastor of a small growing church. I had been blessed to continue to be the father of my own five children that I had raised. I had been blessed to have been the parent of almost 30 other foster children, including another young man who was living in my home that God placed there. I was indeed blessed. I was blessed with a meager amount of income in the way of my Social Security Disability and the meager amount of money that I earned at Youth Advocate Services. I've truly been blessed to have my own home and still be able to live in my own home, instead of staying at a nursing home.

I turned again to Zeta and I said, "To whom much is given, much is required." So upon my return, I rise to the call that you have extended to our church and I accept the challenge to figure out a way to provide some sort of nourishment to the children of Eritrea. I realized that God, if for no other moment in time, had spared my life to hear such a story. And in hearing such a story, I realized that God was going to allow me the opportunity to, in some way, help to raise some food and to provide water for the children of Zeta's hometown of Senafe. I gave him my word in the sanctuary on that Sunday. I asked him if he would forgive me, that I was really leaving town the next day, but upon my return I would embark upon a campaign and I would not stop until the Lord had given me peace in my heart to know that I had done my very best to supply an opportunity for the people of our community to assist the people of his community in some way.

Zeta looked at me as though it was another broken promise that he had heard from countless people before. I don't know whether he believed me in his heart or not. He had been coming to our church for some time and accepted me as his pastor, as his man of God, but I don't know how he interpreted what I was saying. I don't know in his mind if he thought I was just putting him off. Perhaps he had heard that before from other people as he shared his story? Maybe he had heard other people say they wanted to help in some way and maybe raised a dollar or two to send to his community? But I felt the tug on my heart that

God was telling me there was more to be done and more money needed to be raised than just a few dollars to help the children in his country.

On my way out of the sanctuary that day my heart was heavy and I tried to assure Zeta that our church, in some way, was going to be able to minister to his congregation. So it was on that Sunday that we departed. We had mixed emotions. I was excited about the opportunity to go to Guatemala and, yet, faced with another challenge before I walked out of the door.

I remember thinking, "God, I don't know what you're doing to me, but I realize my life is not mine and that it's now changing to be all that you'd have me to be, and to be a minister to as many people as you would have me minister. So, God, I want to rise to the call that you have extended. God, as I sit this on the back burner to go into mission project in Guatemala, I know that when I return home, God, that you will have yet another mission project for me to embark upon."

A dialogue continued in my head: "Tomorrow I leave for Guatemala. Is Africa next? If so, where else must I go? What other missions do you have planned for me, God? Tell me, is the rock that almost struck me down now the cornerstone of my life? How can this be? I'm blind. My face is not the face you gave me at birth, but I know it's your face. Am I wrong to question you? Am I capable of achieving your plan for me? God, help me. ✞✞✞

Appendix

As the Beatles sing,
a group I grew up with...

"I get by with a little help from my friends…"

These are just 3 of many, many people who believe in me & have helped spread this message of forgiveness.

Forgiveness

by Joyce E. Barrie © 2011 Joyce E. Barrie
BlogTalkRadio.com/joycebarrie

How do I forgive?
How do I let go?
You hurt me so bad,
And you know this is so.

How could you, I ask
I am reminded every day
The pain is so intense
It just won't go away.

You really were cruel
What you did was obscene
You left me devastated
How could you be so mean?

When truth be told
I knew that the healing key
Was to forgive you.
Not for your sake--but for me.

And so, I forgive you
But I may never forget
What you did to me
That you don't even regret.

Without this healing
Which is so dramatic
Forever my life would be
Totally traumatic.

And so, I forgive you
Though what you did was a sin
I am forgiving you
So the healing can begin.

And... Now that you've read Joyce Barrie's poem, "Forgiveness," why don't you listen to Joyce herself read it for you?..
www.bit.ly/mTlfhG

"He Lives What Most Of Us Only Preach And Prescribe!"

Stan "Dr Breakthrough" Harris
Breaking 7 bricks

- At age 6 was beaten, tarred & feathered by a teenage gang. He started in Karate to learn how to protect himself, now, out of 7 billion people in the world; he is one of less than 100 who have attained the highest honors, the 10th degree Black Belt.
- He has been inducted into the Black belt Hall of Fame, & Motivational Speakers Hall of fame. He has spoken in all 50 states & 27 Countries earning as much as $47,000 in one hour! He has spoken to crowds as large as 17,000.
- He is an entertaining, enlightening, & electrifying speaker. His life is dedicated to helping you break through every barrier that tries to hinder you physically, emotionally, spiritually or financially.

"Dr Johannes J Christian is a walking message of hope and inspiration! As Dr BreakThrough I often say I can't provide a BreakThrough, I just prescribe it, however when anyone follows my prescription, God almighty provides the BreakThrough that they desire and deserve. Well, the first step of my BreakThrough formula is forgiveness, **and I know of no one who has a more powerful story and life application than Dr Christian.**

Reading, hearing and meeting Dr Christian is an experience that will change your life forever! He lives what most of us of only preach and prescribe!

I urge you to get anything he puts out, and by all means book him to speak for your event or Church - you and everyone who hears him, will be glad you did!" - Stan Harris

- He invites you to watch a short BreakThrough presentation with him breaking bricks at **www.DrBreakThrough.com**
- He also has free downloads at **www.FreeFromDrBreakThrough.com**

Ted Ciuba
Author Bestselling *The New Think & Grow Rich*,
Quantum Business Acceleration Coach

"An instruction manual to consciously direct the Quantum universe to manifest your positive desires"

Discover Ted Ciuba's best-selling personal development book & get $297 in Quantum Business Accelera-

Press Features "Forgiveness"

"Innocent Man Blinded In Senseless Attempt On His Life Demonstrates Power Of Decision"

Columbus OH— The press touts his message of "forgiveness". I see a lot more. It starts with love. And his message, albeit he is Christian and his life *is* a Christ-centered life, isn't about trying to convert anybody. It's not a book about religion, it's a book revealing the heroic human spirit that *somehow* knew life was not over. *Sight is gone*. And a whole string of other inconveniences were suddenly introduced into his life...

There's that famous sonnet of John Milton, British statesperson and poet, afflicted by blindness as a middle-aged adult, who, having discovered patience, concludes, "They also serve who only stand and wait."

But Dr. Christian, though he's certainly become acquainted with patience, isn't waiting about. Anointed in God's lineage, just as he was before the accident, he's out there laboring tirelessly, sharing the message of *The Face Of Forgiveness*.

This is **a spell-binding, heroic drama of turning adversity into benefit.** Through Dr. Christian's noble spirit and decision, **his individual tragedy serves humanity in a broader way.**

This is one of those rare reads, that can literally change your life. I highly recommend it.—Ted Ciuba

Visit...

www.**ThinkRich**.com
www.**QuantumUp**.com

Made in the USA
Charleston, SC
18 December 2013